Contents

WELCOME

My name is Mike Applin and I am extremely excited and proud to be rolling out this business opportunity explaining how to start your own cleaner introduction service, often known as a cleaning agency.

Before I get into the nitty-gritty I want to tell you a little bit about me and how I came to write this book. I'm just a normal guy who left school at sixteen and got a lucky break by joining a large multinational company based in my hometown. To cut a long story short I progressed fairly rapidly through the ranks and ended up a middle manager with 75 people reporting to me.

I enjoyed all the trappings of corporate life with an excellent remuneration package, but at the end of the day I was still at the beck and call of my lords and masters. This involved a lot of travelling round the UK and abroad with my young family which was far from ideal for their education. I think in one particular hectic year my wife and I actually moved house 4 times!

Then one day, almost out of the blue, I had to make a huge decision - my company had decided to outsource many of its in-house activities and I was given the chance to either move to another job 500 miles away or take redundancy. After 24 years I decided to hang up my corporate boots, take the redundancy package and get on with the rest of my life.

A brave new world awaited me but what next? I'm sure a lot of you have been in the same position. I began scouring the various businesses that might suit my talents and came across one that satisfied all the criteria I was looking for:

- Could be run from home
- White collar management in style
- Great income potential
- High profit margins / low overheads
- Growth industry
- Long term clients

That business was running my own cleaner introduction service. I now had two choices; either buy an expensive franchise or research the opportunity thoroughly and go it alone. I visited and talked to several domestic cleaning franchise operations but soon ruled them out because:

- I would have been limited to a specific postcode territory (often not near to where I lived)
- There was a high initial franchise fee
- There were high ongoing monthly management fees
- Overall I would have been restricted in terms of how I wanted to develop the business
- There seemed little brand awareness of these organisations

Over the following 6 months I thoroughly researched how these businesses operated, had meetings with the Inland Revenue to discuss PAYE and NI implications and developed my own marketing and administrative systems.

I am now delighted to bring you all this knowledge at a small fraction of a franchise cost and with no limitation on where you may operate.

But that's not all because I am offering these great additional benefits to give you a flying start:

1) Subsidised Website Offer

I realise that many of my students do not have the time or inclination to build their own website, so we offer a heavily discounted alternative. For only £149 (plus VAT) we can build you a feature rich, custom designed, 11 page, cleaning agency website. This option may be taken up at any time. For further details please visit: http://howtostartacleaningbusiness.org.uk/subsidised-website/

2) Half Price On-line Advertising

Half price advertising in one of the UK's top on-line cleaning directories: http://www.cleaningdirectory.co.uk. The normal cost for 12 months advertising is £99 plus VAT, but I have negotiated a 50% discount, so you get it for just £49 plus VAT. To take advantage of this offer you simply have to email info@cleaningdirectory.co.uk quoting discount reference *GOLDMINE 50.*

3) Trade Price Printing

I provide you with the opportunity to print your business forms and stationery at trade prices, through our trade printers. Just email info@howtostartacleaningbusiness.org.uk when you are ready to discuss your printing requirements. Delivery within the UK Mainland and minor artwork alterations are free of charge.

4) Document Customisation Service

If you are on a low start up budget and cannot afford to have your forms printed externally, you may be interested in our document customisation service. For only £147 (plus VAT) we'll send you downloadable versions of all our business documents and customise them with your company details and logo. This service enables you to open and print your documents from your computer, saving you many hours of work and hundreds of pounds in artwork / printing costs. For more information please visit:
http://howtostartacleaningbusiness.org.uk/document-customisation-service/

If you are motivated, organised and take action I am confident you will build a successful business in the vibrant domestic cleaning sector.

I look forward to helping you on this exciting and profitable journey.

Mike Applin

WARNING AND DISCLAIMER

This book reflects the author's experience of running a cleaner introduction service. There is no guarantee to the income you can derive from this business opportunity as it will depend on various factors including where you intend to trade, the level of competition and what efforts you make. The publisher is not liable for any damages or losses associated with the content of this book.

Every effort has been made to ensure the accuracy of the content of this book, however the publisher and their representatives cannot be held responsible for any errors or omissions.

This document is for information purposes only and does not impart legal, financial or tax advice to readers who must consult their own legal and professional advisors before spending money or taking action of any kind based on operating any business including the business outlined in this report. It is the reader's responsibility to ascertain and abide by national and international laws.

Contact: info@howtostartacleaningbusiness.org.uk

OVERVIEW OF HOW A CLEANER INTRODUCTION SERVICE WORKS

Your Main Roles:

- Finding, vetting and training cleaners.
- Maintaining a database of carefully vetted cleaners
- Attracting, signing up and maintaining clients.
- Allocating cleaners to clients.
- Ensuring your cleaners do not exceed the current financial thresholds for Income Tax and National Insurance.
- Accounting

It's not rocket science is it? Yet clients will pay good money for this service. Don't worry I'm going to show you exactly how this works later in the book.

What Services Will You Provide?

There are many types of cleaning company providing services for the domestic market:

- House cleaners
- Window cleaners
- Carpet cleaners
- Oven cleaners
- Bin cleaners
- Gutter cleaning
- Roof cleaning and so on.

But your Cleaner Introduction Service will focus solely on good old *routine housework*: dusting, polishing, vacuuming, mopping, scrubbing and ironing. To begin with your service will be limited to regular weekly cleans with a minimum of 2 hours per session - this is because your cleaners will want a regular income that they can rely on. As you get bigger with more cleaners on your database you may also consider offering one-off spring cleans and tenancy cleans which attract far greater profit margins.

To keep things simple, when I refer to domestic cleaning from now on I mean regular housework and ironing services.

How Do You Get Paid?

For introducing cleaners to your clients you will receive an ongoing fee, based on the number of weekly hours worked by the cleaner, paid quarterly in advance. You will not have to bother yourself with operating payroll for the cleaners, as your clients become the cleaners' employer and pay them directly each week. But you will have to ensure your cleaners have no other jobs and do not earn more than the current financial thresholds for income tax and national insurance. You will find more details on this topic later in the book.

Here's an example of how much you may earn from a typical client:

Mrs Jones wants a cleaner for 4 hours per week to do general cleaning and some ironing every Thursday morning. You check your records and find that you have a cleaner (Ann) on your books who lives just 1/2 mile away from Mrs Jones and doesn't mind doing ironing as well as cleaning. You arrange for Mrs Jones and Ann to meet and they agree a start date.

Mrs Jones knows that she must pay Ann directly at a rate of £8 per hour and additionally she must pay your company an ongoing fee for finding Ann and for providing holiday and sickness cover. Let's say your hourly service fee is £2.50 per hour, Mrs Jones will pay you £2.50 x 4 (hours per week) x 13 (number of weeks per quarter) = £130.

This one client will be paying you over £500 per year and you don't have to leave your office, do any cleaning yourself or even pay the cleaner! Now imagine having 200 to 300 similar clients generating over £100,000 in income per annum and perhaps you can see the potential of this business!

How To Deal With The 'Red Tape'

Okay, we've established that the cleaners you provide are employed by your clients, not you. This is fantastic as you don't have to pay cleaners and deduct income tax & national insurance. This is a huge administration burden removed from your shoulders, but you must protect your clients by ensuring the cleaners you introduce do not exceed the thresholds set by the authorities for income tax and national insurance (NI). This is what you have to do:

a) When a cleaner applies to register with your company you must get them to sign a Declaration Of Income Form confirming that since last April 6th (the start of the tax year) they have not earned more than the weekly income tax threshold (currently £192 for the tax year 2014 / 2015). Financial thresholds tend to change every year so please visit http://www.hmrc.gov.uk/rates/it.htm for up to date information. Earnings should include any taxable state benefits and allowances:

    - Jobseeker's Allowance
    - Carer's Allowance
    - Employment and Support Allowance
    - Incapacity Benefit
    - Bereavement Allowance
    - Widowed Parent's Allowance

    You are trying to establish that their total income from work, taxable benefits and taxable allowances, before joining your service, does not exceed the current weekly income tax threshold. If it does you should not offer them work in the current financial year, unless they are registered with HMRC as self employed. Universal Credit is not taxable.

b) Ask them to confirm that they are not receiving a state or occupational pension. If they are you should not offer them work, unless they are registered with HMRC as self employed.

c) Ask them to confirm that the work provided by your company will be their only job and that they will keep you fully appraised of any changes. If you provide their only work you will be able to keep track of their total income from clients and ensure that it doesn't exceed NI and income tax thresholds. If they already have a job you will not be able to offer them work unless they are registered with HMRC as self employed.

d) If they want to start another job whilst continuing to receive work through your service you will have to terminate your agreement with them and notify clients because the additional income stream will make it impossible to monitor total income, unless they are formally registered with HMRC as self employed.

e) Put our recommended system in place to monitor cleaners' hours.

I know it may sound a little complicated but it's really not. It's totally necessary to ensure your clients do not have to bother themselves with income tax and NI issues.

To explain why you need to do this we first need to examine the UK income tax and national insurance financial thresholds.

UK Income Tax

Everybody living in this country is allowed to earn a specified amount of money before they have to pay income tax - this is known as a personal allowance. For the tax year 2014 / 2015 the vast majority of the population under the age of 65, the allowance is £10,000 (£192 per week) before paying income tax. The personal allowance threshold does reduce or increase in certain situations, for example if you were employing anybody over 65 or whose income is more than £100,000 per annum. Please refer to the HMRC website (http://www.hmrc.gov.uk/rates/it.htm) for more details.

To keep things simple I would recommend you:

a) Do not register any cleaner with an income over £100,000. What do you think the chances are of that happening!

b) Avoid registering any cleaner who is 65 or older or anybody in receipt of a state or occupational pension. This is not because of age, but because of tax complications. Whilst the personal allowance increases after 65, this is often offset by retirement income which would need to be taken into account. Calculating an individual's income tax and NI liability is complex and confidential, therefore don't even think about trying. Keep things simple and clear cut by following our system.

Finally you should be aware that personal allowance tends to go up each tax year so you will need to update your calculations annually. You can get this information from your accountant or from the HMRC website.

National Insurance

National Insurance contributions are paid to build up an entitlement to certain state benefits, including the State Pension. The contributions paid depend on how much an individual earns and whether they're employed or self-employed. National Insurance contributions stop when you reach State Pension age. The lower earnings limit for employed people (Primary Class 1) is £111 per week for the tax year (2014 / 2015). This means your clients (who are the cleaners' employer for tax purposes) do not have to register with HMRC or pay employers NI contributions if the cleaner's cumulative weekly earnings do not exceed £111 per week. This is most important as the last thing your clients will want is to be burdened with is this red tape. This is why you need to keep a detailed and up to date record of the total hours worked by all your cleaners. Don't worry I am going to provide you with details of the forms you need and how to keep a check later in this book. You should be aware that national insurance thresholds tend to go up each tax year so you will need to update your calculations annually. You can get this information from your accountant or from the HMRC website (http://www.hmrc.gov.uk/rates/it.htm) which shows current rates and information.

To calculate the maximum weekly hours your cleaners may work you simply need to divide the NI lower earnings limit threshold (currently £111 for 2014 / 15) by the cleaner's hourly rate. For example if Cleaner 'A' is paid £8 per hour by your clients, the maximum number of hours she can work is:

111 divided by 8 = 13.

To build a bit of fat into the system in case your clients suddenly increase the number of hours or you want to deploy the cleaner with other clients to cover holidays / sickness, you may wish to set a lower overall limit.

In reality most of your cleaners will not want to work anything like this threshold for fear of losing certain state benefits or because they have other commitments like looking after children or elderly relatives.

On average your cleaners will only have 2 to 3 clients. The average number of hours taken by each client will be 3, so the vast majority of your cleaners will be well below the income tax and NI thresholds. However, if you have a good cleaner who is close to exceeding the above limits, they will need to consider seeking permission from HMRC to become registered as self employed if they want to gain more work through your service. Actually this is not as simple as it sounds because HMRC would apply various tests and criteria to establish whether a cleaner is genuinely regarded by them as self employed. For further guidance on this I recommend you visit their website: http://www.hmrc.gov.uk/calcs/esi.htm. Here you will find an employment status indicator to help determine the cleaner's eligibility to become self employed.

Assuming HMRC is satisfied that the jobs the cleaner does through your service may be regarded as self employment, it is then up to her to review whether or not it would be in her best interests. She may lose certain state benefits and would have to take care of her own tax affairs, which may not suit everybody. There are self employed cleaners out there but they a few and far between. However, once a cleaner is registered as self employed it does take a lot of weight off you and your clients because they can work as many hours as they like as long as they account for the pay they receive to HMRC. It also means the cleaner can work for other clients that she has picked up herself.

Phew, we're through the technical stuff! Now let's look at the types of company operating in the domestic cleaning market.

THE COMPETITION EXPLAINED

When it comes to house cleaning in the UK, the market is mainly served by three types of service provider:

- **Private Cleaners ('Mrs Mops')**
  These are normally informal single person operations, who agree to clean your home for a 'cash in hand' arrangement. They will not usually offer any insurance cover and any pre-vetting will be down to the client.

- **Domestic Cleaning Companies With Direct Employees**
  These may range from small operations to Limited companies employing hundreds of people; they may also be part of a larger cleaning franchise operation, for example *Molly Maids*. There will normally be a formal contract in place between the client and the cleaning company. The work is usually billed on scope rather than actual hours worked and the client may not have the same cleaner(s) at each visit as they tend to work in flexible cleaning teams. The cleaning company is responsible for paying their cleaning team and for taking care of PAYE and NI requirements. Insurance is usually provided but the scope may vary widely.

- **Domestic Cleaning Agencies or Cleaner Introduction Service (as we prefer to be known)**
  Essentially cleaning agencies work as brokers by putting cleaners in touch with clients. They charge an agency fee for finding the cleaner, which is usually levied on hours worked; for example if a client uses their nominated house cleaner for 3 hours per week, they would pay the agency their agreed hourly fee x 3. Additionally the client would directly pay the cleaner what is due to them. Don't worry if this sounds confusing - all will be explained later in the book. Usually the agency will vet cleaners, supply cover for holidays and may also provide a degree of insurance, but rarely fidelity insurance to cover possible theft. Domestic cleaning agencies may be part of a larger cleaning franchise operation such as Time For You.

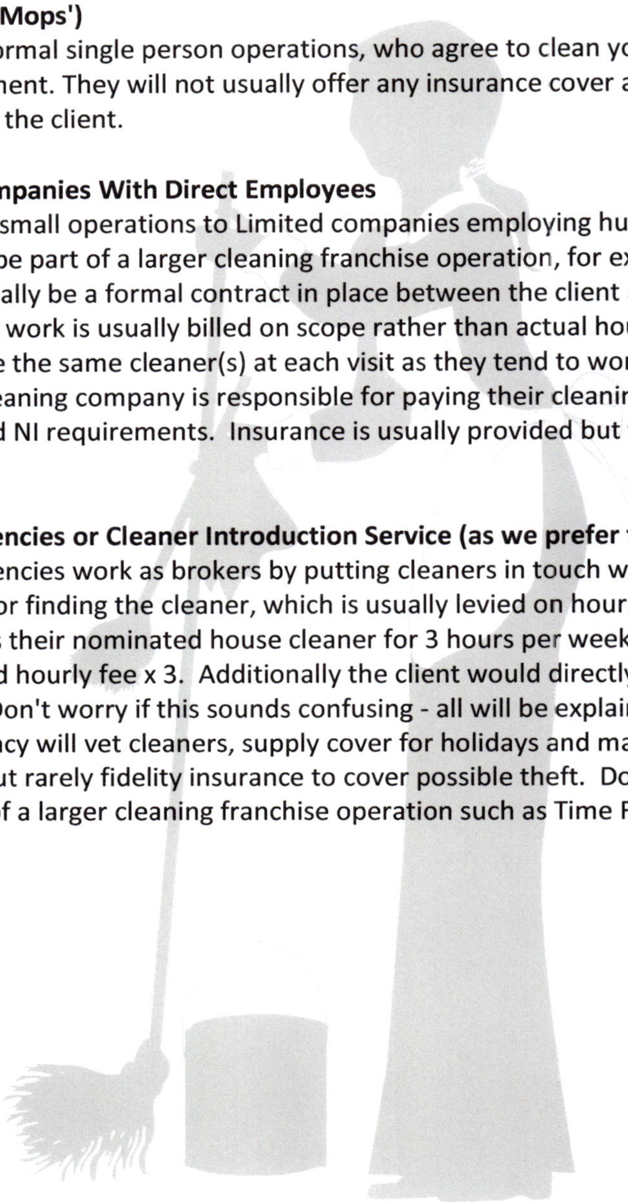

Your Service Versus the Competition

What Advantages Will Your Service Offer Over Domestic Cleaning Companies With Direct Employees?

PRICE:

Domestic cleaning companies with direct employees have significant overheads including:

- Company vehicles
- Fuel and servicing of vehicles
- Staff uniforms
- Cleaning equipment
- Cleaning materials
- PAYE and NI burdens
- Offices
- Franchise fees (if applicable).

Your cleaners will make their own way to the clients you assign to them.

The cleaning equipment and materials will be provided by the client.

There will not be any PAYE or NI burden as your cleaners are employed by your clients, not you. You do not require rented offices as you will operate from home.

The bottom line is that you can significantly undercut these companies on price.

SAME REGULAR CLEANER:

These companies work in teams so there will usually be 3 people cleaning different areas of the client's house at any one time. Some clients would find this intimidating, particularly if they are at home when the cleaning takes place. Also the constituent members of the team often change so continuity may suffer. Most clients prefer to build up a rapport over time with a single cleaner.

IRONING:

It is rare for these companies to provide ironing as well as housework services. Many people hate ironing more than housework, so you will offer this additional benefit.

What Advantages Will Your Service Offer Over Private Cleaners?

CONTINUITY OF SERVICE:

Private cleaners are by definition 'one woman' bands so if they go on holiday or become sick there is no cover. You will provide holiday and sickness cover if your clients require it.

VETTING:

Clients feel embarrassed and do not have the time to carry out detailed vetting of cleaners. You do reference and character checks for them and replace cleaners that clients are not happy with.

INSURANCE COVER:

Private cleaners rarely have any kind of insurance cover but you will safeguard your clients by having liability insurance in place to cover major damage or injuries.

What Advantages Will Your Service Offer Over Domestic Cleaning Agencies?

IMAGE:

Some clients do not like dealing with ‘Agencies’, so we use the term ‘Cleaner Introduction Service’ as it is fresh and better describes the service provided.

PRICE:

The majority of domestic cleaning agencies you come up against will be part of a bigger franchise. Every month they will have to pay out management fees to the franchisor that you won't. Some franchisors even set the agency and cleaner rates which takes control away from their franchisees. This means you should always be able to undercut them on price.

YOUR PERSONAL SERVICE:

You are what sets you apart from other agencies in your area. If you demonstrate commitment and professionalism to your clients and cleaners you will win and retain business.

HOW BIG IS THE DOMESTIC CLEANING MARKET AND IS IT RESILIENT?

Putting an exact figure on industry turnover is difficult given the scale of the black market and the dearth of published research on it. However, some industry experts estimate the domestic cleaning market may be worth around £2.86 billion in the UK, with some 2.5 million households being amenable to or employing some sort of help in the home. Let's face it there are 25 million households in the UK, so demand for domestic cleaning services will always be high.

The sustained growth in demand for domestic cleaning services in recent years is due to a number of socio-economic factors:

- Increased disposable income levels, particularly among dual-income households.
- An increase in the numbers of women employed outside the home.
- Far greater focus on leisure over domestic responsibilities (the live hard, play hard ethos).
- An increasing social acceptance of having help in the home. This is now seen as a status symbol rather than a stigma.

It seems that cleaning services are always in high demand, even in recessionary times, with many clients regarding help with the cleaning as a necessity rather than a luxury. Here is a non-exhaustive list of the type of customers you will want to target to build up a successful client-base:

WHO NEEDS YOUR SERVICES?

For most people, the daily grind doesn't inspire them to want to do the household chores of when they get home at the end of a stressful day.

- **Young Professionals and Double Income Couples.**
  Today's professionals often work long and stressful hours, with little time for leisure and relaxation, leaving no desire to spend what little free time is available cleaning the house. Commuter towns or residential areas close to city centres are a rich source for this type of client.

- **Mums with Young Children**
  This portion of the market is large, however opportunities for custom may be harder to find as disposable income can be lower within this group. It is also worth noting that young mums will usually have a network of friends that are also young mums, so it may be possible to boost your reputation and gain promotion through word of mouth.

- **Senior Citizens and Disabled People**
  For obvious reasons this demographic may find it difficult to carry out the cleaning on their entire property, so need a helping hand with some of the more arduous tasks. Many older clients also like to have a cleaner because it provides them with a bit of company.

- **Single Men**
  Notoriously uninterested in the cleaning process, single men are a good source of clients.

- **Privileged Individuals or Families**
  Usually living in affluent areas, this group has larger than average disposable income and are the kind of people that would admit they enjoy being pampered. They are normally highly sociable people, which is beneficial in spreading your reputation.

- **People Moving House**
  A lucrative sideline to regular cleaning are one off cleans.
  Typically tenants of rented property require this service at the end of the rental period in order to secure the return of deposit monies held by estate agents.

SETTING UP THE BUSINESS

Okay you now have an overview of how this business works and who needs your services. Now let's turn our attention to setting up the business for your particular circumstances. I know you will probably be raring to get going but first I urge you to spend time planning your business and setting it up correctly. The work you put into this phase will more than pay dividends later so make sure you cover all the bases.

1) Market Research

You need to find out who your competitors are and how much they charge for their services. This will provide valuable information about how much you need to pay to attract cleaners and how much mark up you can make. From this you will be able to draw up a Schedule of Charges. Obviously, you will need to compile your own schedule based on the market research you carry out in your area. A sample is shown below:

Sample Schedule of Charges

Required Weekly Hours	Cleaner Rate Per Hour	Your Fee Per Hour	Total Hourly Rate	Your Weekly Fee	Your Quarterly Fee
2	£8	£2.50	£10.50	£5.00	£65.00
2.5	£8	£2.50	£10.50	£6.25	£81.25
3	£8	£2.50	£10.50	£7.50	£97.50
3.5	£8	£2.50	£10.50	£8.75	£113.75
4	£8	£2.50	£10.50	£10.00	£130.00
5	£8	£2.40	£10.40	£12.00	£156.00
6	£8	£2.30	£10.30	£13.80	£179.40
7	£8	£2.20	£10.20	£15.40	£200.20
8	£8	£2.10	£10.10	£16.80	£218.40
9	£8	£2.00	£10.00	£18.00	£234.00
10	£8	£1.90	£ 9.90	£19.90	£258.70
11 or more	£8	£1.70	£ 9.70		

Note that you can state that your rates start from £9.70 per hour. Okay, the client would have to take 11 or more hours but it's still a valid statement. The vast majority of your clients will want 4 hours or less, therefore you should include your top rate at these levels. You should keep a copy of your schedule by your phone so that you can quickly calculate the hour rate should clients ask for a specific number of hours. I also keep a copy with my client presentation so that I can quickly complete the Client Agreement and Standing Order Mandate.

Finding your competitors is easy; just carry out a Google search for terms like: domestic cleaning, house cleaning, home cleaning, domestic cleaning agencies etc, all followed by the town you want to target. For example domestic cleaning Brighton, house cleaning Brighton and so on, if Brighton was your target area. If you are targeting a big city such as London, you should break your search down into smaller population areas, for example Hampstead, Wimbledon etc.

If you are looking to cover more than one town or area repeat the process for the additional places. Here is an extract of what Google brought up for the search 'domestic cleaning Brighton':

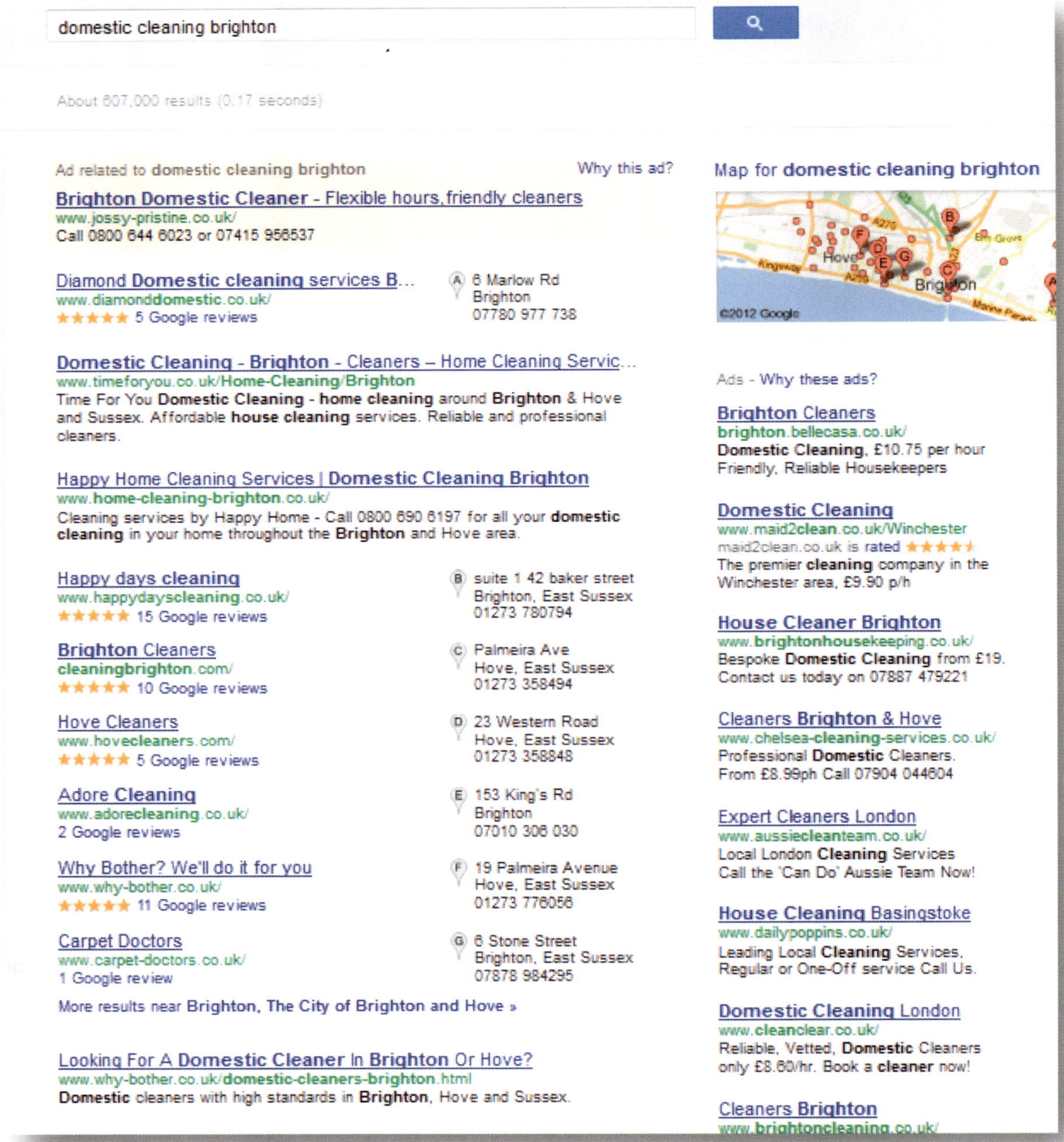

After a while you will start to recognise the domestic cleaning franchise operations such as: Time For You, Bella Casa, Maid 2 Clean, etc, who will be your direct competitors in the agency market. Don't forget that you should be able to undercut these companies as they have to pay management fees to the franchisor every month. You will also start to recognise national domestic cleaning companies who directly employ their staff, for example Daily Poppins can be seen in the results above. Don't forget these companies have big overheads so again you should be able to substantially beat them on rates.

You can also find your competitors in local newspapers either promoting their cleaning service or advertising for cleaners.

Now take the information you have extracted from the internet and local newspapers and compile a table. Spreadsheets are great for doing this and easily updated. Here's the detail you should include if possible:

Company Name	Telephone Number	Website Address	Cleaner Hourly Rate	Agency Hourly Rate	Overall Hourly Rate	Minimum Weekly Hours	Ironing Yes/No	Comments

Obviously the size of your competitor list will vary depending on the size of the population area you have targeted. Now start to research the following information:

I. how much your competitors charge
II. the 'going' hourly rate for cleaners in your area
III. the minimum number of hours you can contract the cleaner per week (usually 2 or 3)
IV. do they offer ironing services

If your competitors are cleaning agencies you should be able to find out the hourly rate paid to the cleaner, the hourly agency fee and the overall hourly rate. If the competitors are not agencies they may quote a rate per hour or are more likely to quote a rate per job, which means you can usually discount them as being uncompetitive.

How can you find this information out I hear you asking? Well, first of all get as much information as possible from your competitors' websites, and then call them as a bogus customer. I usually make up a story about an elderly aunt who now needs help with housework and possibly ironing because of failing health. I say that at this stage I'm only calling to get a feel for how much a regular cleaning service will cost and how it works. This prevents them having to visit auntie's house, which embarrassingly does not exist!

To find out if they are an agency I'll say something like 'would my aunt pay the cleaner every week or does she pay you?' If they say they need to see the property before they can quote then they are probably a cleaning company employing their own employees.

The bottom line is you need to find out the hourly rate (including the agency / cleaner rate break down if they are an agency), the minimum number of hours 'your aunt' can take per week and whether they provide ironing services as well. A lot of companies will open up and tell you all sorts of addition detail so make a note as you go through.

The first call you make will probably feel a bit awkward but after a while I'm sure you'll slip into Laurence Olivier mode to find out all you need to know. Have fun - all's fair in love, war and business!

If you are more confident and have the time to do it you could say you want a cleaner for your own home. Tell them that you and your partner both work and need a regular weekly clean. Then when they come round you can pick their brains. This can be quite valuable as you can see how they actually present to clients - you might be surprised how poorly a lot of companies do this.

The other thing that might surprise you is the number of companies who you cannot get through to or do not return calls / emails. This should give you a lot of confidence because if they are thriving on such poor customer service, just imagine what you will achieve!

At the end of your market research you will be fully aware of what you will have to pay to attract cleaners and how much of a margin you can make per hour. This information should be fed into your business income and expenditure budget (see below). You will also know your competitor strengths and weaknesses which is invaluable when you meet with clients.

2) Preparing a Business Income & Expenditure Budget

Why do you need to do this? Well imagine trying to manage your household expenses without knowing what you expect to earn or pay out. It's no different for a business.

The Start-Up Budget:

a) Stationery and Business Forms:

A list of forms and stationery you will need to run your business are detailed in the Appendices. Appendix G covers items that we recommend you may print internally on a laser or ink jet printer. Appendix H details items that should really be printed professionally either because they are legal documents, multipart forms or given out to clients and cleaners.

We have arrangements with trade printers that can provide extremely competitive prices for your forms and stationery, particularly if you order them at the same time and use our existing artwork with only minor modifications. I have detailed the discounted prices for you in Appendix H. If you want to place an order, have any printing questions or want further quotations please don't hesitate to email info@howtostartacleaningbusiness.org.uk

The Low Cost Document Customisation Option:

If you are on a really tight start-up budget it is possible to make do with single part forms which you would have to either fill in twice, use carbon paper or copy. For example the Client Agreement is a 2- part form (one for you and one for the client).

To cater for those students on small budgets or short of time we offer a document customisation service.

We can add your company name, address, telephone number, email address and company logo (if you have one). We then supply you with customised files so you can open and print them on your own computer / printer.

The cost for this optional service is **just £147 plus VAT**, which is incredible value when you consider that we have to alter nearly 30 documents. For more information please visit: http://howtostartacleaningbusiness.org.uk/document-customisation-service/

b) Office Equipment:

- Desk and Chair
- Personal Computer
  This is not essential to start with but it is highly recommended as you grow your business.
- Word processing and spreadsheet software.
  If you can't afford Microsoft products you can download excellent free software from http://www.openoffice.org/ .
- Laser Printer
  You can pick up really good printers nowadays for less than £50.
- Landline telephone
  A dedicated business phone is recommended but not essential at the beginning. As you get busier I would certainly recommend having 2 business phones: one for cleaner enquires and one for client enquires.
- Mobile phone
- Calculator
- Filling cabinet or shelves
- Stapler
- Lever arch files
- Hole punch

When you first set up your business your budget may be limited, but many of these items are already available in the average family home.

c) Public Liability Insurance Premium

Please refer to the Insurances section for more information. You should allow between £300 to £400 depending on the extent of the cover provided and the excess that applies. The excess is the amount of money you agree to deduct from the cost of any claim.

The Ongoing Budget:

Now you a have a handle on how much it will cost to set up the business, you should then turn your attention to ongoing costs and draw up a budget for this too. This should include:

- **Local Newspaper Advertising**
  Primarily you will use local newspapers to find cleaners and promote your services. You will find more information on this later in the book.

- **Printing and Distribution of Client Mailers**
  I am referring here to postcard sized marketing literature that will be dropped through letterboxes in targeted areas. Initially you will deliver these yourself but as you get busier you can hire somebody to do your distribution or use a reliable distribution company. You will find more information on this later in the book.

- **Newsagent Window Advertising**
  This is a good and relatively inexpensive way to find cleaners. You will find more information on this later in the book.

- **Online Promotional Costs**
  I am primarily referring to costs associated with promoting your business online. One of the advantages of buying my book is that we have negotiated a half price advertising deal in one

of the UK's top on-line cleaning directories: http://www.cleaningdirectory.co.uk. The normal cost for 12 months advertising is £99 plus VAT, but you get it for just £49 plus VAT. To take advantage of this offer you simply have to email info@cleaningdirectory.co.uk quoting discount reference: *GOLDMINE 50.* I also provide you with a subsidised website building option, where we'll set everything up for you for £147 (plus VAT).

- **Vehicle Fuel and Servicing**
  Obviously you will need to visit clients and cleaners so you need to factor in this extra cost. If you live in London or one of the bigger UK cities you may be able to make do with public transport but be sure to include this extra cost in your budget.

- **Office Consumables, Printing and Postage**
  External printing costs should not be significant in the first 12 months, as your first batch of business forms and other printed stationery items (recommended in Appendix H), should last you at least one year. Alternatively, you may have opted to print all your forms internally, using our document customisation service mentioned earlier, in which case you simply need to allow for the cost of toner and printing consumables.

- **Business Insurances**
  These are usually due annually but you may find some brokers / companies that allow you to pay monthly. This is an ongoing cost that you need to allow for. Never trade without at least having public liability insurance.

We've looked at expenses but now we need to look at the exciting bit...........

How Much Income Do You Want To Generate?

You need to decide how quickly you want to grow your business. Domestic cleaning agencies can be run part time or full time - it's up to you and your personal goals. The more hours you put in the more income you will generate. This will be determined by how much marketing you do and how quickly you can find suitable cleaners. If you want to generate a turnover of £50,000 within 12 months, you can calculate how many clients you need as follows:

1) First work out your average weekly income per client by multiplying the average number of weekly hours per client (usually 3) by the service fee you want to charge per hour (say £2.50). In the above example your average weekly income per client will be will be £7.50.

2) Next calculate the average yearly income per client by multiplying the average weekly income per client (see above) by 52. So in this example it is £7.50 x 52 = £390.

3) Now divide your annual turnover target (£50,000) by your average yearly income per client to work out how many clients you need to generate. Again, let's use the above figures:
50,000 / 390 = 128 clients.

This means you would need to sign up about 10 or 11 new clients per month to hit your target. To service this number of clients you're going to need to recruit about 3 to 4 cleaners per month. I believe that breaking things down into mini goals like this makes them much easier to understand and achieve. If your goal was to generate annual revenue of £25,000 then you would only need to sign up 5 to 6 clients per month and recruit 2 to 3 cleaners. The great thing about this business is that you set the agenda!

To summarise, you should now know how much your business will cost to set up and the monthly running costs. You also know the expected income on a month by month basis (don't forget that clients pay you quarterly in advance which is great for cash flow). If you subtract predicted costs from projected income it will show you immediately when you will start to make profit. With such relatively low start-up costs it shouldn't take too long to become profitable, providing you take action and follow my recommendations.

3) Choosing an Effective Business Name

A business name is more important than most people give credit especially when it comes to the cleaning sector. Unfortunately some business proprietors let ego get in the way and name their businesses after themselves. This is fine if they are a renowned world authority on domestic cleaning, but I wouldn't say there are many of those! A good business name actually has the power to draw business in its own right. For example which of these businesses would you choose if you were looking for a domestic cleaner?

A.P. Smyth and Sons OR *Domestic Cleaning Angels*

I rest my case. Apologies if either of these are real companies.

Creating an effective business name needs a little bit of thought but it really is important. If you start with a poorly chosen name you'll put yourself at a disadvantage. It's like running a marathon in wellington boots; you'll get to the finish if you try but a lot slower than the competition.

I'd recommend using a brainstorming session with friends and family to come up with a list of names. Don't rule anything in or out, just go with the flow. Then filter the names through these tests:

- **I.** Is the name memorable? You need people to remember it and recommend you.
- **II.** Is it easy to spell? You need people to find you in directories and online.
- **III.** Is it easy to say? You need to effortlessly answer the phone so don't go for a tongue twister.
- **IV.** Does the name convey a positive emotional feeling? Put yourself in the clients shoes - what are they looking for: clean fresh, tidy, freedom......
- **V.** Does the name encompass what you do? You only get a few seconds to make an impression with your marketing material so choose wisely.
- **VI.** Does the name represent a key search phrase in Google. We cover this in more detail later in the book.
- **VII.** Is the name short and to the point? Don't ramble on.
- **VIII.** Does the name conjure up a visual image? When people read your company name will they mentally associate it with an image? This makes it easier to remember and links back to the positive emotional feeling aspect. Good examples of this are Orange (mobile network) and Apple (computers).
- **IX.** Does somebody else already use that name? If somebody else is already trading with your shortlisted name then eliminate it to avoid possible legal issues. You don't want anybody suing you for infringement of trademarks or passing off.

You should now have a name which passes the above tests and you are happy with. If you are really stuck for ideas look at what the bigger players are called and use that for inspiration.

4) Choosing a Business Bank Account

When you start a business it is important for accounting purposes that you keep you private transactions separate from your business transactions. Therefore I recommend that you open an independent business bank account in your company's name. There are a great many banks vying for your business so choose wisely. Much of your income will be received by standing order payments so look for a bank account that minimises the charges on this aspect. If you are short on cash you may need to select a bank that offers reasonable overdraft facilities. Also look for banks that offer free banking for 12 months, which could be important to you during the start-up phase. Whatever you do, choose a bank that you will be happy dealing with for the foreseeable future. The last thing you want to do is change banks as this would require you writing to all your clients asking them to change their standing order mandates - remember you are providing a service to lighten their load, not increase it! Don't give them a reason to cancel.

5) Deciding On Your Businesses Legal Entity

Let me issue a warning in advance - this section is a bit dull and technical but it is important so please don't be tempted to skip it. As if you would?

This section of the book does not constitute legal or financial advice as I am not a lawyer or an accountant. However, I want to make you aware of the different legal statuses your business can trade under. In the UK a business can be classified as a sole trader (one person owns the business), partnership (two or more people own the business), limited partnership (LLP) or limited company (Ltd). Why is it important to choose the right sort of legal entity? Well, let's imagine one of your clients decides to pursue a legal claim against your business because of a major problem that has occurred due to the cleaner's negligence. In reality this would be difficult to prove if you have vetted the cleaner properly and have appropriate insurances in place. However, if you want to give yourself total peace of mind the best course of action is to limit your financial liability. This can be done by making your business a limited company or limited partnership. This means that the company becomes a legal entity in its own right and any claims would be against the company's finances, not your personal assets. These limited liability arrangements may also offer tax advantages in some situations.

The downside with limited liability arrangements is that there is a cost to set them up and a requirement to submit annual accounts to Companies House. In short there is more red tape which will cost you more money in accountancy fees and bureaucracy. However, if you are looking for peace of mind against possible financial claims you should certainly consider this option. For more information I recommend you seek advice from your accountant or visit the Companies House website at http://www.companieshouse.gov.uk/about/guidance.shtml . There is also an excellent article on this website: http://www.whatbizopp.com/mark-business/2582-how-to-form-a-limited-company.

6) Writing Your Contract Forms

Your business will have two prime contract forms:

I. Client Agreement
This contract defines the agreement that exists between you and your client. It spells out the precise service you will provide and how much the client will pay you for that service.

II. Cleaner Terms of Association
This contract defines the agreement between you and your cleaners. It explains the exact nature of the arrangement between you and the cleaner and your obligations to one another.

Why are these forms so important? Well in essence they provide protection in the event of legal disputes. For example, suppose one of your clients tries to strike up a private arrangement with her allocated cleaner, by cutting you out. One way to prevent this is to predefine in the client contract the level of compensation if this happens. In fact good contracts should actually prevent the need for litigation because responsibilities and actions are clearly defined from the outset.

Further guidance on compiling your own terms and conditions is provided later in the manual.

7) Insurances

Public Liability Insurance

Before you start trading you must take out public liability insurance. This provides cover for personal injuries and damage caused by the negligence or omission of your business and your registered cleaners, for which you can be held legally liable.

You need to decide on the level of cover you require, with public liability cover of £1 million per claim being the minimum. Please note that policies are offered with varying levels of 'excess'. This means the first part of any claim would be borne by you and the balance paid by the insurance company. Expect to pay more for lower excess levels.

Here's an example of how a claim might work in practise. Let's say one of your cleaners breaks an expensive ornament (worth £500) whilst she is cleaning a client's home, so you check your insurance policy and find you have an excess of £100. If a claim is made under the policy, you will pay the first £100 (the excess) and the insurance company will pay the remaining £400 to settle the claim.

You also need to be aware that some policies may come with exclusions, for example bleach damage. Some policies even exclude the item being cleaned, so if an ornament is dropped whilst being cleaned it is not covered, but if the dropped ornament falls on another item and causes it to break, the item it falls on is covered.

Top Tip: Don't just focus on the premium cost. You must always consider the level of excess and any exclusions.

Top Tip: Make it clear in your Client Information Booklet what is covered and also what is not covered by your insurance policy.

Remember that public liability insurance acts as a safety net for major claims. It is not really there for minor breakages, therefore the client may be persuaded to claim on her own household insurance which could have a lower excess. In this situation I would recommend you consider paying all or part of the excess if you sense the client is unhappy. This could be given as a fee payment holiday until the amount is cleared.

Another reason for providing public liability insurance is for marketing purposes. You will find many companies use the term 'fully insured' in their advertising material without defining what 'fully' means. In my experience clients rarely ask about insurance and get confused about different types of cover.

If the agent wants to know how many workers you have on your books please ensure he is aware that they are part-time workers and ask if he wants it converted to full time equivalents.

Let's assume that your part-time workers work an average of say 7 hours each, that would mean that if you had 5 workers it would equate to one full time employee (7 x 5 = 35 working hours per week). As you build the business you should keep the insurance company informed of numbers based on your actual figures. Otherwise there is a risk that they may only pay a proportion of any claims because you under reported the number of full time equivalent workers.

Employers Liability Insurance

This type of insurance covers claims for bodily harm or death to employees during the course of their employment. Anybody employing staff must have employers liability insurance. Your client legally employs the cleaner therefore they should cover this risk, by making sure their household insurance policy covers domestic employees. You should point this out to your clients and help them to check their policy, if required. Many household policies cover this risk with a level of cover up to £10 million. To cover any possible gap in the clients' insurance policy and also for marketing and cleaner recruitment reasons you may decide to provide employers liability insurance. Some brokers may offer public liability insurance with employers liability insurance - this is known as combined insurance.

Fidelity Insurance

One type of insurance you are unlikely to offer is fidelity insurance. Fidelity claims originate from acts of employee dishonesty, forgery, robbery, computer fraud, embezzlement, counterfeiting and a number of other criminal acts.

As the cleaners are not technically your employees you may be hard pushed to get this type of cover which is very expensive anyway. Be aware that some cleaning companies (usually the ones who employ cleaners directly) do offer this but in my experience clients rarely ask about the possibility of theft by a cleaner. If it does come up I'd say something like 'we vet the cleaners by asking for references and checking where they live. If money or valuables were to go missing they would automatically come under suspicion so it would be absolutely stupid of them to steal from you'. This normally sets their mind at rest.

8) Appointing an Accountant

Unless you are a whizz with double entry book keeping and filling in tax returns I would recommend you get yourself a qualified accountant.

They will be able to advise you on how to record income and expenditure, recommend accounting software and keep you up to date on income tax and NI thresholds so you can update your forms and systems accordingly. A good accountant needn't cost the earth and should be able to save you money by knowing how to account for things like depreciation of assets and how much to claim for use of your house as an office etc. Try to find one that has a good fit to the type of business you run and particularly knows all about taxation issues with regards to the employment niche you will be operating in. For example, it may be an advantage to pick an accountant that has a cleaning agency on its books.

If you are going to become a limited company or limited partnership I believe it is a requirement for a qualified accountant to prepare and sign off your accounts.

PRE-LAUNCH ACTION PLAN

1. Read this book until you thoroughly understand the concepts.
2. Follow the guidance for setting up your business shown earlier in the book.
3. Set up your office, business email account and telephone(s). Remember if you are short of funds you can use your home telephone / mobile to begin with.
4. Decide on your business name.
5. Decide on your target area(s).
6. Carry out your market research to assess viability.
7. Draw up your schedule of charges.
8. Decide what legal entity you will trade under (sole trader, partnership, limited company). Be aware that Limited Companies can take weeks to set up.
9. Prepare your income and expenditure budgets.
10. Open a business bank account.
11. Consider using our subsidised website building option, but please allow up to 5 days for us to build your site.
12. Consider using your half price advertisement on http://www.cleaningdirectory.co.uk after your website has been set up.
13. Research and take out your insurance cover, with a policy start date to match your launch.
14. Write your Client and Cleaner Agreements and consult with a lawyer as necessary.
15. Design your client marketing material or use one of the specimens provided.
16. Order your client marketing materials (takes about 5 working days).
17. Sort out your other printed items (forms, contracts, information booklets etc). We provide you with various options within this book.
18. Set up your spreadsheets or hard copy documents for Client Records, Cleaner Allocation Records, Cleaner Weekly Earnings Schedule and Fee Payment Schedule.
19. Set up your accounting software or manual accounting books.
20. Research local newspapers and place your advertisements to recruit cleaners and attract client enquiries.
21. Design and print off your cleaner recruitment cards or use one of the specimens provided.
22. Research local newsagents and place your cleaner recruitment cards in their windows.
23. Place your cleaner recruitment cards on local notice boards.
24. Set up your filing system.
25. Deliver your client promotional cards in your target areas, or get someone to do the distribution for you
26. Be prepared to take customer enquiries (have the Client Enquiry forms ready on your desk)
27. Be prepared to take cleaner enquiries(have Cleaner Telephone Pre-vetting forms on your desk)
28. Rehearse your client presentation, client enquiry script, cleaner enquiry script and cleaner meetings.
29. Familiarise yourself with all your agreements and forms and practice filling them in.
30. Celebrate your successes – treat yourself for each important milestone that you achieve (for example: first client sign up, first cleaner recruited)

It sounds a lot of work but if you are sufficiently motivated you could have everything completed and ready to earn your first income within a couple of weeks. Remember there's always lots of work setting up any new business, but once you have launched you will reap the benefits of planning and implementing this phase correctly. Many of the steps outlined above can be carried out simultaneously, whereas others need to be completed in sequence, for example you can't print your standing order forms without knowing your new business bank account details.

Pre or Post Launch:

- Set up your free Google Places advertisement. We can do this for you for £49 plus VAT.
- Set up your free Facebook Page.
- Research and appoint an accountant.
- Gradually introduce other forms of advertising for clients and cleaners as mentioned earlier in the book.

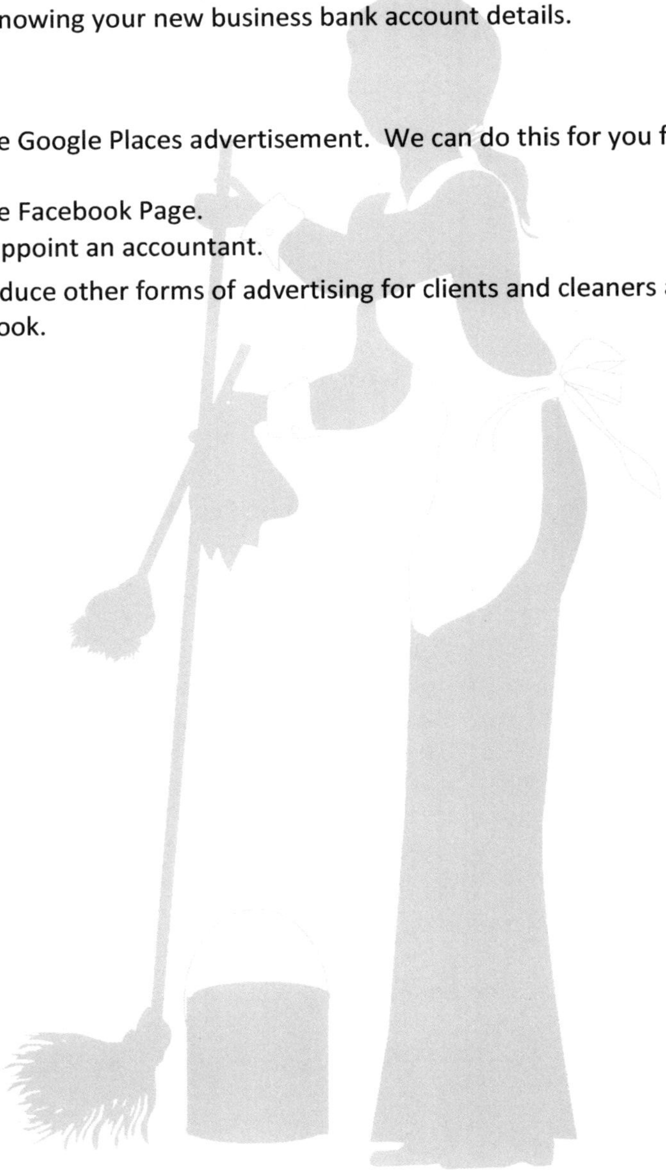

EVERYTHING YOU NEED TO KNOW ABOUT CLEANERS

This is probably the most important part of book because your business hinges on supplying honest, reliable, pre-vetted part-time workers. Don't be tempted to take short cuts with the recommendations in this book or there is a high probability that you will end up with egg on your face!

What Motivates People To Apply For Domestic Cleaning Jobs?

Let's face it cleaning someone else's house is not most people's idea of having fun or a fulfilling career. Yet there are some people out there that are very happy to be cleaners. What motivates them to do it? Let's look at some of the factors that may influence them:

- **Money**
  They need money to supplement the household earnings. This might be for a holiday, treats for the kids or just making ends meet.

- **Part Time**
  We are offering part time work which suits people who have to juggle running a home or picking up the kids from school.

- **Cash in Hand**
  Your cleaners are paid in cash by the clients you allocate to them, so there is no need for a bank account or having to work weeks before they get paid.

- **High Unemployment / Competition For Jobs**
  We live in times of high unemployment which makes it difficult to find regular work. You'll be surprised how many of your cleaners hold qualifications but have been unemployed for some time.

- **Cleaning Isn't Rocket Science**
  Nearly everyone can quickly be taught to clean providing they are physically fit, methodical and motivated.

- **Boredom / Sense of Purpose**
  Some people hate to be stuck indoors with nothing to do; they get bored and need to feel they have a purpose.

- **Recognition**
  We all love to be praised and it is no different for cleaners. For some cleaners it means the world to hear their clients say 'I don't know how I would cope without you'.

- **Dislike of Supervision**
  Many cleaners like the freedom of carrying out their work without a boss to answer to. Okay, the client is their immediate boss but they are often out of the house when the cleaner calls or just let them get on with things.

Who Wants To Be A Cleaner?

- Young mums whose children are at nursery or school.
- Mature women whose children have left home.
- Older women who can't find other work because of their age or lack of qualifications.
- Bored housewives.
- University students and young people trying to find their first job.

How To Find Cleaners

There is no shortage of people looking for the type of work you can offer, but your job is to find *suitable* applicants. The bad news is that on average for every 10 cleaners that make contact with your business, you will usually end up with 1 cleaner on your books. This is due to the necessary pre-vetting and filtering processes that exist to weed out unsuitable applicants. We cover this in a lot more details under the Cleaner Vetting section. Even when you think you have found a suitable cleaner they may leave at short notice because they don't get on with the client or just decide cleaning isn't for them. Why am I telling you this? Well I want you to understand that building your database of reliable and vetted cleaners is first and foremost a numbers game. It's like prospecting for gold - if you keep sieving you will eventually end up with golden nuggets. **These will be the cleaners that stick with you for years and become the bedrock of your business.**

There are many ways to advertise and find cleaners:

Local Newsagent Windows

This can be a good way to generate responses from a particular area. The rates may vary between 50 pence to a couple of pounds per week / fortnight. Here is an example of cleaner recruitment card:

Top Tips:

a) In our experience this can be a little hit and miss, so keep records of where your responses are coming from so you can eliminate the newsagents that are not generating any leads.
b) Once you know the outlets which are generating a steady flow of leads you should try to renegotiate the rate with the proprietor. Ask them what discount they will give you to advertise for a longer period, say one month or more. Your aim should be to reduce the rate by half, but if the agent usually has a full window this may be difficult to achieve.
c) Ask the newsagent to position your advertisement at eye level if possible. Ads placed at the bottom of the window are less likely to be read.
d) Try using luminous highlighter on your ad to make it stand out.
e) Don't use your company name in the ad. Try to make it sound as it's a family looking for a cleaner.
f) Experiment with using handwritten cards as this can work better in some areas.

Local Newspapers

Compile a list of the local newspaper titles for the area(s) you want to target. Some of these will be free newspapers and some readers will have to pay for. Now go to the Job Recruitment section and take down the details of who to call at the newspaper if you want to place an advertisement.

Newspaper	Telephone	Contact Name	Distribution	Circulation	Rate	Comments

One thing you may notice is that some of the contact telephone numbers are the same. This is because many titles are owned by bigger groups. When you call you need to explain that you are just setting up a business and need some information. You need to find out the following:

- **The Distribution**
  This is the area that the newspaper is delivered to or sold in, which should be broken down by town and postal districts, for example RH10 = Crawley. This information is important to you because you want to have a good match between the area(s) you cover and the newspaper's distribution.

- **The Circulation**
  This is the number of copies distributed on average per period of time. In the case of local newspapers this is normally weekly. Circulation is one of the main factors used for setting advertising rates. Circulation is normally audited by independent bodies for

example ABC (Audit Bureau of Circulations) which provides a degree of comfort that the particular newspaper does indeed reach the number of people claimed by the publisher.

- **The Advertising Rates**
  Ask the sales team to send you a 'rate card' which will detail out the cost of advertising per title under their control. With bigger publishers they may offer a rate for advertising in more title in their stable.

  Top Tips:

  a) As with all advertising, you need to be able to pick out what works and what doesn't so when cleaners call you must try to find out where they saw your ad.
  b) Drop any newspaper media that is not working for you.
  c) Ask for discount if you commit to advertise for longer
  d) Ask if the newspaper will run your press release for free if you advertise with them.
  e) Find out the deadline for advertising copy. If you call them near to that time they will often slash rates if they have space to fill.

Local Church, Parish or Village Magazines
This can be an inexpensive and targeted way to find cleaners. Contact the publishers, who might just be volunteers and tell them you are just starting your business. Ask if they can offer a special rate or suggest they come back to you if they have space to fill just before publication. You will be surprised how much discount you can get.

Word of Mouth
Word of mouth is a free and underestimated way to grow the number of cleaners on your books. Ask your friends and family to put the word out for you and make sure you tell everyone you meet that you are looking for good cleaners. Word will soon get round and it will pay dividends.

Recommendations From Your Existing Cleaners
Ask your cleaners if they know anybody who might want a job. This can be extremely powerful because they have first-hand experience of how your service operates and they are extremely likely to know people in a similar position as themselves. They can act as fantastic 'recruitment sergeants' for your business. I would go as far as offering them an incentive of say £20's worth of Marks & Spencer's vouchers for every cleaner they introduce to you that you start.

Nursery and Pre-School Groups
This can be a great place to find young mum's with a few hours on their hands who want to earn extra cash.

Immigrant Groups / Societies
The amount of immigration into the UK in recent years is well documented, particularly from eastern Europe Providing they can speak English to an acceptable standard, immigrant workers can make excellent cleaners. Just make sure you check their right to work in the UK.

Your Website
If you choose the subsidised website option, I provide you with a dedicated cleaner recruitment page.

Local Clubs & Groups

If you think there are local clubs or groups that may contain potential cleaners then ask them if you may display your cleaner recruitment card on their notice boards.

Public Notice Boards

If you have public notice boards in your area ask if you can add your card.

This above list is not meant to be exhaustive. Apply a bit of lateral thinking to your own area and you will probably find additional local places to advertise.

How To Vet Cleaners

Vetting cleaners for suitability is a 3 stage process:

1) Telephone Pre-Vetting
2) The Cleaner Interview
3) Reference Verification

Telephone Pre-vetting

Telephone pre-vetting is the process of carrying out a structured initial assessment of the cleaner's suitability. I recommend you use a Cleaner Telephone Pre-vetting Form which serves 3 purposes:

I. It provides a permanent record of potential cleaners that you can use for follow up purposes.
II. It provides a script to keep you on track in terms of covering everything and controlling the conversation.
III. It highlights early on the suitability of cleaners so that you can end the call quickly if necessary. After all time is money and you don't want to miss the next cleaner call because you are caught up with a non productive prospect.

You may feel more comfortable coming up with your own form and script but here's one I would recommend:

CLEANER TELEPHONE PRE-VETTING

DATE: ____________

WHERE DID YOU HEAR ABOUT US?
NEWSPAPER / MAGAZINE / POST CARD / REFERRED BY / OTHER

HAVE YOU WORKED AS A PAID CLEANER BEFORE? YES | NO → POSSIBLE PROBLEM

CAN YOU PROVIDE 2 CHECKABLE REFERENCES? (EMPLOYER / CHARACTER). YES | NO → CAN'T USE

CAN YOU CONFIRM THAT YOU HAVE NOT EARNED MORE THAN £ PER WEEK (INSERT CURRENT INCOME TAX THRESHOLD) FOR THE CURRENT TAX YEAR, FROM 6TH APRIL. YES | NO → CAN'T USE

HOW MANY HOURS DO YOU WANT TO WORK PER WEEK? IF MORE THAN 12 HOURS IT COULD BE A PROBLEM UNLESS THEY ARE SELF EMPLOYED.

DO YOU HAVE YOUR OWN TRANSPORT? YES | NO

WHICH AREAS ARE YOU PREPARED TO TRAVEL TO FOR WORK?

PLEASE COULD I TAKE YOUR CONTACT DETAILS:

NAME:
ADDRESS:
POSTCODE:
TELEPHONE NUMBER:
MOBILE NUMBER:
AGE:
NATIONALITY: (If not an EU National, you need to see their work permit / right to work documentation).

NOW LET ME TELL YOU ABOUT US AND WHAT WE DO.
We are a family business that finds cleaners for local families needing help with their housework. Our clients will pay you in cash at a recommended minimum rate of £ per hour.
How does that sound? Do you have anything you want to ask me about the job? OK, I just need you to put a few things together and then we can arrange to meet up. Have you got a pen handy? We need:

2	CHECKABLE REFERENCES (FROM PREVIOUS EMPLOYERS / CHARACTER REFERENCE)
1	FORM OF ID (PASSPORT / DRIVING LICENCE / BIRTH CERTIFICATE)
1	ADDRESS VALIDATION - A RECENT UTILITY BILL (GAS / ELECTRIC / TELEPHONE) OR BANK STATEMENT WITH YOUR NAME AND ADDRESS ON IT.
2	PASSPORT PHOTOS (BADGE / FILE)

You sound just like the type of person we are looking for so please call again when you have got everything together.

MEETING AT CLEANER'S HOME SCHEDULED FOR:

COMMENTS:

Let's take a look at how a typical cleaner pre-vetting enquiry might go. I've also explained why we ask certain questions. Make sure you fill the form in as you deal with each enquiry and then file them for future reference, either by area the cleaner lives or alphabetically or whatever way you feel most comfortable with.

The phone rings and you answer **'Good morning, this is (insert name), how may I help you?'**
Your tone should be welcoming and friendly.

The cleaner will probably say something like' I'm ringing about the cleaning job'

You reply **'Oh that's great, can I take a few details from you please'......**

'Where did you see the advert?'
You are trying to find out the source of this enquiry because you need to know what advertising works and what doesn't. Over a period of time you'll see clearly from the forms where your leads are coming from and hence you can adjust your advertising spend accordingly.

'Have you worked as a paid cleaner before?'
You are asking this question because experienced cleaners are more likely to be better at it and you should be able to get references from previous clients.

If they say no, it's not the end of the world but you would have to ask them if they have done housework before to find out how good they may be. Perhaps they clean their own house so you'll be able to check this when you visit their house to interview them.

'Can you provide 2 checkable references?'
You are looking for them to provide:

- **2 previous employer references**
  Ideally these will be from previous cleaning jobs, but this is not essential.
  or
- **1 from a previous employer and 1 character reference.**
  or
- **2 character references** (if the prospect seems good in all other respects).
  Character references should be from respected sources.
  For example: Health Visitor, Vicar, Teaching Professional, Doctor or similar.

'Can you confirm you haven't earned more than £181 per week since 6th April?'
If they have had a previous job paying more than £181 per week you can't use them for reasons explained earlier (see pages 10 and 11)

'How many hours do you want to work?'
If they say they want more than the maximum limit you set (to keep them under income tax and NI thresholds) you must say the best you'll be able to offer them is 12 hours or whatever limit you set. If they are happy with that you may continue. If they are not happy with that they would have to consider applying for self employment status with HMRC or you can't offer them anything. The number of hours is normally not a big issue as most cleaners only want up to 10 hours per week anyway.

'Do you have your own transport?
You need to find out how the cleaner will get to the clients you assign to her. If she has a car, scooter or even a push bike it is a big advantage. Having said that, if public transport is good in the area being covered, say a big city, this can be another solution providing fares are reasonable. If the cleaner is relying on walking I would advise limiting her clients to within a 15 minute walk maximum.

'Which areas are you prepared to travel to for work?'
This is a neat way of knowing how far the cleaner is prepared to travel for work and makes the process of matching clients to cleaners so much easier. Ideally your cleaners should be relatively close to her clients; however when you first start out this may be difficult to achieve.

'May I please take your contact details?'
This allows you to keep in contact with your prospective cleaners and build a rapport with them whilst they sort out their paperwork. Also it may highlight that they live in a notorious area - I know it's not nice to generalise and pigeon hole people but forewarned is forearmed.

Age?
Why do you ask their age? For 2 reasons:

- It can prompt us to ask if they are in receipt of an occupational or state pension, which probably eliminates them because of the reasons given earlier in the book.
- If the applicant is young you need to check what experience they have had and whether they have the necessary maturity for the job. Our experience of students is that they tend to be unreliable and do not stick around for long.

Nationality?
Nationals from EU countries have automatic right to work in member countries. Currently these include: Austria, Belgium, Bulgaria, Croatia, Cyprus, Czech Republic, Cyprus, Denmark, Estonia, Finland, France, Germany, Greece, Hungary, Ireland, Italy, Latvia, Lithuania, Luxembourg, Malta, Netherlands, Poland, Portugal, Romania, Slovakia, Slovenia, Spain, Sweden and the UK. If your cleaner does not have UK nationality you will need to see their passport to verify their ID.

Additionally if the nationality of your cleaner is not shown above you will have to ask for proof that they have permission to work here i.e. a work permit. If they do not have the necessary documentation you must not use them.

Now tell them about your service and sell the benefits. Ask if they have any questions and deal with them courteously and honestly. A common misconception cleaners have is that your involvement somehow reduces their pay. You must explain to them that you actually negotiate some of the best rates for your cleaners and only place them with suitable clients so saving them having to look for work.

Now tell them the documents you require them to put together and why you need them.

- References to show the standard of their previous work and to verify their character.
- ID to prove who they say they are.
- Address validation to prove that they live at a specified address.
- Passport photos for their identity badge and for your internal records.

Tell them that you have to take these simple precautions to protect your clients who are just private householders. They should have no problem with this if they are motivated, want the work and have nothing to hide. In fact if they can't be bothered to do this imagine how reliable they would be if you were to allocate them to clients. This process has the added benefit of seeing how much they really want the job!

If they pass this initial telephone pre-vetting stage say something like:
'You sound just like the sort out person we are looking for and I am looking forward to having a chat once you've got your documents together - just call us when you have'.

Now you are more than half way to registering another cleaner on your database, who could earn you £1300 per year if they perform just 10 hours work per week for your clients.

Top Tip: Treat good cleaners like royalty as they are twice as hard to recruit as customers!

If you do not hear back from cleaners and a client comes up near to them you may wish to give them a quick call to encourage them. You might say something like this:

'Hi (use their first name), this is just a quick courtesy call to let you know we have found a client looking for a cleaner in your area (tell them roughly where). I wondered how you are getting on with putting together your paper work.' You'll soon get a feel for whether they are really interested and you can then push for an early meeting so as they don't miss out on the opportunity.

The final box on the form is for Comments. Use this to record your initial gut feelings, for example you might write something like: 'Ann comes across as articulate, friendly and really wanting work' or 'Sue comes across as a bit surly and disorganised' or 'Katrina's English is not very good - this may represent a possible communication problem' . Remember these are only initial reactions but often first impressions are accurate. When you are perhaps receiving 10 cleaner enquiries a day you'll find it difficult to remember each individual call so every little bit of information helps to form an opinion.

Finally if somebody calls 'on behalf' of a cleaner just end the call very quickly by saying:
'Thank you for calling but can you please ask your (wife, niece, mother, friend) to call me directly.'
You do this because you want to make sure the individual is not being coerced and can speak English which is essential for good communications with you and your clients.

The Cleaner Interview (First Meeting)

You have asked cleaners to put their paperwork together and then call you back. When they do you will need to dig out their original Telephone Pre-Vetting form and complete the final section which records when you are going to meet up. But before you do I recommend that you remind them of the specific documents you are looking for:

2	Checkable References (from Previous Employers / Character Reference)
1	Form of ID (Passport / Driving Licence / Birth Certificate)
1	Address Validation - A recent utility bill (gas / electric / telephone) or bank statement
2	Passport Photos (Badge / File)

In addition, if they are not an EU national they will have to provide you with evidence of their right to work in this country.

Once they have confirmed that they have everything you would say something like 'Thanks for putting all that together, it's really appreciated. We want to find you work as soon as possible so when would be a good time to meet up for a quick chat to move things along? '
Please note that I don't say 'interview' as this would put a lot of cleaners off. I recommend you keep it informal sounding.

When the subject of venue is raised I'll say something like 'To save you time and travelling expenses I'll come to your house'. Of course you're scheduling the meeting **at the cleaner's home** for three reasons:

- To carry out the interview and check their documentation.
- To verify that they do actually live there.
- To secretly assess the standard of the cleaner's own housework.

When you arrive at the cleaner's house introduce yourself and try to put them at ease by making some small talk. Then thank them again for taking the time and trouble of putting the paperwork together. I usually say 'we've just got a few bits and bobs to sort out, it shouldn't take longer than 20 minutes to half an hour, is that okay?' Why are you asking permission? Well, it makes them believe they are in control as some people may feel intimidated by having a stranger asking them questions in their own home.

I would recommend that you start the interview by recapping what you told them during the telephone pre-vetting stage:

- Explain how your service can be a big advantage to her. You're going to find families in her local area who need help with the housework with hours that fit in with her schedule.

- Explain that before you can offer her work you need her to:
    - Complete an application form (see specimen form below).
    - Confirm her previous income was below £181 per week (see specimen form below).
    - Provide a work permit (for non EU nationals only).
    - Provide two checkable written references.

- If you are just starting out you must be fair to the cleaner and tell them that you do not have any immediate clients in her area, but after her references are verified, you will make it a priority to find her work as quickly as possible. See 'The Client / Cleaner Conundrum Section for useful start up strategies.

Top Tip: See 'The Client / Cleaner Conundrum' Section for useful strategies for dealing with this problem.

Now you've set the scene it's time to begin an informal interview process. Firstly check her paperwork is in order. To assist you with this I recommend you use the Cleaner Interview, Vetting & Training Record shown below or something similar. This form is basically a check list, to make sure you cover everything at the first and second meetings with the cleaner.

CLEANER INTERVIEW, VETTING AND TRAINING RECORD

APPLICANT : ______________________________ **DATE:** ___/___/___

PROOF OF IDENTITY:

Passport / ID CARD / Photo Driving Licence / Original Birth Certificate		
Nationality:	Doc. No.:	Expiry Date:

PROOF OF ADDRESS:

Gas / Electricity / Telephone / Bank Statement / Water Rates / Council Tax Bill
Dated: / /

FIRST MEETING (Cleaner Vetting) :

References Provided?	
Application Form Completed / Signed?	
Income Declaration Signed?	
Passport Photographs provided?	
Work Permit? (for non EU Citizens)?	

SECOND MEETING (Cleaner Training) :

Terms of Association signed?	
Worker Information Booklet explained?	
Cleaner Weekly Earnings Declaration explained?	

COMMENTS / ACTIONS:

Let's look at how this form is filled in:

Proof of ID
Tick one of the options and record the relevant details.

Proof of Address:
Tick one of the options and record the date of the document. The must be within the last 3 months and be in the cleaner's name.

First Meeting (Cleaner Vetting):
Tick off the details as you go through and add any relevant comments .

Second Meeting (Cleaner Training):
Complete these details during the second meeting.

Comments / Actions:
Make appropriate notes as you conduct the vetting and induction

If something is missing or does not tie up you should either eliminate the cleaner as unsuitable or return when she can provide complete and valid documentation. If the documentation tallies up you should take away the 2 checkable references plus the 2 passport photos. Also for non EU nationals you should take away a copy of the right to work documentation or ask that this be made available when you next return.

Next ask the cleaner to complete a formal application form (see below):

Cleaner/Ironer Application Form

About You:

Name: ______________________
Address: ______________________
____
______________ Postcode: ____________
Do you have your own transport? Yes ☐ No ☐
Do you have an answerphone? Yes ☐ No ☐
Weekly hours available to work?: ____________

Home Tel. No: ______________________
Mobile Tel. No: ______________________
Nationality: ______________________
Date of Birth: ______________________
I am available to work in the following areas:
____
____

Using the chart below please tick the times you are **able** to work.

Hours	Monday	Tuesday	Wednesday	Thursday	Friday	Saturday	Sunday
Morning							
Afternoon							
Evening							

Are there any periods in the year (eg. school holidays) when you are unable to work? Yes ☐ No ☐
Have you ever been convicted of a criminal offence? Yes ☐ No ☐
If Yes, please provide dates and convictions below:
____
____

Do you give us permission to run a Criminal Records Check on you? Yes ☐ No ☐

About Your Previous Employment History:

Have you worked as a paid cleaner before? Yes ☐ No ☐ Please provide brief details below:
____
____
(Continue on reverse, if required)

Have you previously provided ironing services to clients? Yes ☐ No ☐
Please provide contact details of two people with whom we may take up references:

Name: ______________________
Address: ______________________
____
______________ Postcode: ____________
Day Tel. No: ______________________
Evening Tel. No: ______________________

Name: ______________________
Address: ______________________
____
______________ Postcode: ____________
Day Tel. No: ______________________
Evening Tel. No: ______________________

Declaration:

I declare that I have answered all questions honestly and fully.

Signed: ______________________ Date: ____________

PHOTO

ALL INFORMATION WILL BE TREATED IN THE STRICTEST CONFIDENCE

I recommend you pre-fill a lot of these fields using the information contained in the original Telephone Pre-Vetting form. This will make the process faster and less intimidating for the cleaner. I also make the point of asking the cleaner if she wants me to complete the application form on her behalf - let's face it we all hate form filling! Just get her to sign it at the end.

All interviews will be different depending on the level of information already provided. As you go through ask questions to clarify any vague or missing information and make appropriate notes. You need to find out what motivates your cleaner.

Next get the cleaner to complete and sign a Declaration of Income Form. This is to confirm that she has not exceeded the income tax threshold (currently £181 per week for the tax year 2013 / 2014). If necessary please refer back to the earlier section which explains why this is necessary. I usually put the cleaner's mind at rest by saying 'this is just for our records; we don't send this to the tax people'.

A specimen Income Declaration form is shown below:

DECLARATION OF INCOME

Title: **Mr** ☐ **Mrs** ☐ **Ms** ☐ **Other** ____________

First Name(s): ____________
(In full)

Surname: ____________

Address: ____________

Postcode: ____________

Date of Birth: / / **National Insurance Number** ____________

Since last April 6th, have you earned more than £192 per week? Please include any taxable state benefits and allowances. (For example: Jobseeker's Allowance, Carer's Allowance, Employment and Support Allowance, Incapacity Benefit, Bereavement Allowance, Widowed Parent's Allowance. YES ☐ NO ☐

Are you receiving a state or occupational Pension? YES ☐ NO ☐

I confirm that I have answered each statement truthfully and will keep your company fully informed of any changes.

I confirm that any work provided through your company will be my only job.

I undersrtand it is my responsibility to arrange my own tax affairs.

Signed: ______________________ Date: __________

Print Name: ______________________

Don't forget!

1) The income tax threshold usually changes each year, therefore you need to insert the new earnings limit at the beginning of each new tax year.

2) You need a 'No' to both the above questions, before you can consider giving her work. In rare situations the cleaner may say she is officially recognised as a self employed cleaner by HMRC. When this happens I recommend that you get her to complete and sign a Declaration of Self Employment. A specimen form is shown below:

DECLARATION OF SELF EMPLOYMENT

Title: **Mr** ☐ **Mrs** ☐ **Ms** ☐ **Other** ________________

First Name(s):
(In full) ________________

Surname: ________________

Address: ________________

____

____

Postcode: ________________

Date of Birth: / / **National Insurance Number** ________________

I confirm that I am officially recognised by HM Customs and Revenue as being a Self Employed Cleaner. I understand that it is my responsibility to arrange my own tax affairs.

I confirm that the above statement is true and will keep your company fully informed of any material changes to my circumstances

Signed: ________________ Date: ________________

Reference Verification

The cleaner should have now provided you with either:

- 2 x previous employment references
- 1 x previous employment reference + 1 x character reference (from a reputable source)
- 2 x character references (from reputable sources).

Firstly read all references to get a feel for their authenticity and the degree of praise given by the referee.

You must now quickly verify the references by sending out a reference request letter. Why do we do this? Well, it has been known for cleaners to forge references or pass off references given to other cleaners as their own. Also, some references may not be all they seem. For example, perhaps a client wanted to get rid of the cleaner and sweetened the pill by giving her a glowing reference when one wasn't due. By writing to them separately you are more likely to get an accurate and honest assessment.

Depending on the urgency and the amount of contact information given, you should write, email or telephone the referee to confirm the references given. My preference is to send a hard copy letter as this is likely to have more validity in the eyes of a client, than an email or notes taken of a telephone call. When sending a hand written reference request be sure to include a stamped addressed envelope to facilitate its return. You'll get far more responses when you do.

If you are short of time you can always send your reference request letter by email as an attachment for the referee to complete and send back. If you are really desperate you could telephone the referee and complete the form yourself with a suitable annotation that this is what happened and why. For example the referee might be just about to start a four week holiday or cannot write because of a hand injury.

Never be tempted to offer an un-vetted cleaner to a client as that could be regarded as negligence on your part if anything goes badly wrong, like theft of the client's property or damage to their home. You must always give yourself the protection of having at least 2 vetted references on file, which the client had the opportunity to view before taking on the cleaner.

If referees do not reply in a timely manner you should not hesitate to courteously chase them up by telephone as the cleaner may find other work whilst you're waiting for their replies.

When you receive back the completed reference requests you must verify that the referee has confirmed the cleaner to be **honest, reliable and satisfactory** in their work. If they are not willing to do this it puts a huge question mark over the cleaner and I would recommend you do not put them on your database.

Finally always treat references in the strictest confidence and certainly never divulge to any cleaner the specific reason(s) you have not given them any work. If asked, simply say you don't have any work in their area at the moment.

The reference request letter should be sent under your company letterhead. Specimen text is shown below:

Mrs A Smith
10 The Place
The Town
The County
The postcode

Dear
Subject:-

The above named person has applied to us for employment as a domestic cleaner and has given your name as someone who may be willing to provide a reference. The position requires total honesty and a high level of reliability.

The applicant will also be expected to demonstrate sufficient responsibility to perform their duties without supervision. Our clients will entrust their keys to the applicant and expect them to turn up at hours determined by them to clean and iron in their private residences.

We would be most grateful if you would answer the questions below and return this form to us in the enclosed reply paid envelope.

When was the Applicant employed by you? From: ________ To: ________

Position Held: ________

Reason for leaving: ________

Was he/she: Honest Yes ☐ No ☐ Reliable Yes ☐ No ☐ Satisfactory Yes ☐ No ☐

Please advise further details:-

____

____

With what level of responsibility was he/she entrusted?
(For example handling cash, keys, stock and any other position of responsibility)

____

____

Signed: ________
Position in company: ________
Name of company: ________

Address: ________
____
____

If we take on this applicant and one of our clients wishes to seek an independent reference from you would you be amenable to such a request? Yes ☐ No ☐

Thank you in anticipation of your early reply which will be treated in the strictest confidence.

Yours faithfully

Add Your Company Name

Cleaner Training and Induction (Second Meeting With Cleaner)

After you happy with the cleaner's references you should organise a second meeting with her which will cover the following training and induction areas:

1) Worker Information Booklet
2) Terms of Association
3) Cleaner Weekly Earning Declaration

Worker Information Booklet

The Worker Information Booklet is an invaluable tool for training and inducting your cleaners into your company's way of working. It also forms part of the agreement with the cleaner as it contains instructions on how they should act. You should develop your own booklet which reflects how your own business operates or you can use the one we provide as Appendix B.

To prevent any misunderstanding I recommend you go through it point by point with the cleaner and invite her to contact you if she needs to clarify anything at any time. Let's take a look at the detail:

Our Role

What we say in the booklet:

In simple terms our main function is to match people who need cleaners with people who want to work as cleaners. Therefore, we act as a 'middle man' serving both clients and cleaners. It is our clients who pay for our ongoing service through an agreed standing order fee. This ensures that if a cleaner goes on holiday, is sick or decides to leave, we will quickly find them a replacement from our database. The monthly retainer paid to us does not impact on your rate of pay. In fact we realise how important it is to retain workers so we have negotiated with our clients what we believe to be some of the best cleaner rates of pay in the market place today.

Why we say it:

You want to remind cleaners of the role that your business fulfils. You want them to know that the fee you charge the client does not impact on their rate of pay. In fact it is in the it's your best interests to suggest high rates of pay to clients because you want to attract and retain good cleaners.

Worker Selection

What we say in the booklet:

We value our reputation and that is why we take time to carefully vet all workers wanting to register with us. By now you should already be aware that we have asked you to provide a lot of information:

- Proof of Identity
- Proof of Address
- Written References
- Passport Photographs

Why we say it:

You want cleaners to feel they are associated with a well run cleaning services business and that they are special.

Placement with Clients

What we say in the booklet:

After successfully completing our vetting procedures we will do our best to place you with clients that match your profile in terms of:

- Number of hours you want to work per week.
- Particular days and times you are available to work.
- Places you are prepared to travel to for work.

We will either allocate you to existing clients, whose cleaners have left, or new clients who wish to try our services.

As you prove yourself we will endeavour to find you as much work as you wish.

Why we say it:

You want cleaners to know that we are taking time and trouble to match them according to the hours they can work and location. You also need to dangle the 'carrot' of more work if they perform well.

Arranging the Initial Client Chat

What we say in the booklet:

ARRANGING THE INITIAL CLIENT CHAT

We will provide you with the contact details of the client and ask you to set up a mutually convenient time to visit them for an initial chat. This will give you both a chance to see if it 'feels right' and will also provide an opportunity for the client to explain her particularly requirements. Nine times out of ten a start date will be agreed on this day and you simply need to advise us.

In the unlikely event that this particular client is not for you, please let us know straight away what the problem is and we will arrange to place you elsewhere.

Why we say it:

You are actually explaining the client/cleaner interview process without calling it an interview. Most cleaners are put off by this word as they may have been rejected at previous job interviews. You are also making it clear that they should contact the client to set up the meeting which avoids a lot of admin work for you. Though you are doing this, you must always ensure that the cleaner actually does ring the client.

When To Contact Us

What we say in the booklet:

You may contact us at any time on (add your phone number here). Our normal hours of business are 9am until 6pm, Monday to Friday. If we are unable to answer when your call, please leave a message on our Answer phone, giving your name and contact telephone number, and we will return your call as soon as we can. It is essential to keep us informed in the following circumstances:

- You agree to change your hours with a client.
- You are feeling unwell and cannot attend work.
- You want time off (please give us and the client at least 7 days notice and ask the if they want a replacement whilst you are away).
- You have an accident whilst working in the client's home, which causes damage to their property or injury to yourself or others.

- The client encourages you to leave us and instead work for them directly. This would represent a breach of contract so please let us know in order that we may diplomatically nip it in the bud.
- You want to increase the number of hours that you work.
- The client is not paying you on time.
- You change your address or telephone number.
- Any other situation you feel we should be aware of.

It is in our interests that you are a success and we will do all we can to support you with clients, so please do not hesitate to contact us if you need help or advice.

Why we say it:

- You need to be aware of the cleaner's hours changing for Income Tax and National Insurance reasons and also to amend the standing order payment for your services fee, if it is going to be a permanent change.
- You need early warning if your client needs a replacement cleaner to cover sickness and holidays.
- You need to be aware of potential insurance claims, particularly if they are major.
- You must take action if the client is trying to poach the cleaner so you can nip it in the bud by reminding them of the terms of your agreement, which allows for substantial compensation if this were to happen.
- You must act on the cleaner's behalf if the client is not paying her on time. They often rely on the money and an unhappy cleaner is likely to leave at short notice.
- You need to be able to contact your cleaners at short notice, so it is essential that any change of telephone number and / or address is notified promptly.

Employment Status and Pay

What we say in the booklet:

You are employed by our clients who are responsible for:

- Setting your work routines.
- Agreeing the times and days they wish you to work, including the total number of required weekly hours.
- Paying you directly in cash at the agreed rate, at the end of each session, or as agreed with you.

You are not employed by us; therefore, we cannot be responsible for your pay. However, whilst you are working for our client(s) you must abide by our Terms of Association.

It is your responsibility to arrange your personal tax affairs. For your information we have included some useful financial information at the end of the guide.

Why we say it:

To re-enforce to cleaners (and also the tax authorities if they ever carry out an audit) that you are not their employer. It also makes clear that the cleaner is responsible for her own tax affairs. She cannot hide behind you or her clients if she has not made a full disclosure of earnings.

Holidays

What we say in the booklet:

It is extremely important that you let us **and** clients know if you want time off. Please give at least one week's notice and ask the client if they want a replacement whilst you are away. If they do, please let us know straightaway so we have sufficient time to organise everything,

Why we say it:
All part time workers are entitled to holiday pay so it is a legal obligation for your clients to pay their cleaners accordingly. Further useful information can be found at the following websites:

http://www.direct.gov.uk/en/employment/employees/timeoffandholidays/dg_10034642

and

http://www.businesslink.gov.uk/bdotg/action/layer?r.l1=1073858787&topicId=1079427399&r.l2=1073858926&r.s=tl

Holiday pay can be a bit of a thorny subject but most clients and cleaners take a pragmatic view because of the low number of hours worked per week. You will find that they usually come up with their own arrangements and only need to become involved if there are disputes or difficulties calculating what is due.

Sickness and Unavoidable Absence
What we say in the booklet:
If you are feeling unwell or need to take time off (for example a family emergency) please notify us and clients as soon as possible. This will enable us to put cover in place, if required by the client. Please note that it is not a requirement for clients to provide sick pay.

Why we say it:
You need early warning to be able to liaise with your client and find out if they require a replacement cleaner. You are also reminding the cleaner that they are not entitled to sick pay (because they earn less than the National Insurance threshold).

Cancellation Gratuity
What we say in the booklet:
We recommend to clients that they pay a cancellation gratuity (non obligatory) whenever they give workers less than 24 hours notice that they wish to cancel a planned work session. Whilst this is usually rare, it does sometimes happen that a client forgets to alter arrangements or inadvertently double locks a door. In this type of situation they should pay you £5 for your wasted time).

Why we say it:
It is only fair that your cleaner receives compensation if the client cancels at short notice. If this occurs more than twice a year you must remind the client that her cleaner relies on the income.

Leaving Us
What we say in the booklet:
Please give us a **minimum of one week's notice**. This will give us a reasonable chance of finding a suitable replacement for our clients. Please don't feel awkward or embarrassed if you want to leave, we promise to accept your decision in a friendly and professional way and besides you may need a reference from us at some time in the future.

Why we say it:
You need as much advance warning as possible if a cleaner is intending to leave especially if they have multiple clients. By reminding the cleaner that they may need a reference she is likely to give you the required one week's notice and hopefully more. Early warning will also give you the opportunity of trying to change the cleaner's mind by finding out why she is leaving. It may be as simple as asking clients to pay her a little bit more to match another offer she has had.

Key Security

What we say in the booklet:

One of the first things you will need to do with new clients is to agree how you should access to their property. If the client is usually out during the day, they will probably want to hand over door and security keys (if appropriate). To protect the interests of clients and workers we recommend that you both complete a Key Security Deposit Form (copy available upon request) that confirms the agreement you have made with the client for the transfer of keys. To ensure there is an incentive for workers to hand back keys when they stop working for clients, we recommend that the client take a small deposit (say £10), which is immediately refundable when the keys are returned. This deposit may be paid in cash or more usually deducted from your first week's earnings. For security reasons client keys must be kept in a safe place at all times and you must not write the client's name, address or telephone number on the keys or key ring. When you leave the clients employment you must hand the keys back in person.

Why we say it:

Managing the return of client keys can be a big administrative time eater unless you provide a means to manage it. When cleaners leave clients they often feel embarrassed, so the physical return of client keys can become an issue. The key deposit system provides an incentive for the cleaner to hand back the keys in an orderly fashion.

Cleaner Earnings Receipt Record

What we say in the booklet:

We have provided clients with Cleaner Earnings Receipt Record forms. This is a two-part form to record earnings you have received with that particularly client. This eliminates the need to rely on memories as it records hours you have worked and most importantly the pay you have received or you are owed. You should complete the first and last sections, with the client completing the middle section. This must be done at the end of each working session. When the form is full the client should sign at the bottom and give you the second copy for your records.

Why we say it:

This form is vital for keeping the record straight between the client and the cleaner but it also serves a more important purpose as the tax authorities would consider it to be an auditable record of hours worked in the client's employment. For this reason you tell the client that they must keep a copy for a minimum of 6 years. This document is also used by you to monitor exact hours worked by the cleaner to confirm the right amount of services fees are being paid and additionally to calculate rebates due to the client if you were unable to provide a cleaner for some weeks. There is more information about this later in the book.

Getting the Best from Your Clients:

Task Lists

What we say in the booklet:

On your first visit to a client, ask them to walk you through their home describing what they would like done on a room by room. We have provided a Task List (see above) for this purpose. We recommend that clients not only complete the Task List but also talk you through how they want things done. It is also important that you ask the client to point out any cherished or valuable items that they do **not** wish you to clean.

Why we say it:
This form is a great way for the client to tell the cleaner what she wants done and what she doesn't want done. It eliminates the need for memory. There is more information about this later in the book.

Cleaning Equipment and Products
What we say in the booklet:
The client is responsible for providing you with all necessary cleaning equipment and products. All equipment is different so please ask them to show you how their equipment works e.g. how to change hover bags. Also ask them to show you where the cleaning products are stored and how and where you should use them. If you feel the client is not providing the necessary cleaning equipment or products for you to do your job properly, then don't be afraid to diplomatically bring it to their attention. Obviously you will get much more done in the time available if they provide the right tools for the job.

Why we say it:
One of the reasons you can undercut your competition is because your clients are responsible for providing the cleaning equipment and products. For the cleaner to be effective the client should provide appropriate items for the job and instruct her in their use if necessary. Where clients are not using the right equipment we encourage them to bring this to the attention of their clients. For example some cleaners may consider it unreasonable to get down on their hands and knees to scrub floors when it has become acceptable to use a mop.

Priorities
What we say in the booklet:
On some occasions there may be more tasks on the task list that can be comfortably managed in the allotted time. In these situations ask the client if she wants to prioritise the tasks, so that the more important tasks get undertaken in the time available. Alternatively they may decide they want you to work more hours. Please always inform us if your hours are increased or decreased by the client.

Why we say it:
Some clients ask for 2 hours cleaning per week but when the cleaner arrives they give them so much work that it couldn't even be covered in 4 hours. The cleaner needs to manage unreasonable client expectations by asking them to set the highest priorities.

Security Systems
What we say in the booklet:
It is important that your client instructs you how to activate / deactivate the security system if they expect you to work in their home whilst they are out.

Why we say it:
This is obvious but sometimes overlooked.

Safety Precautions and General Conduct:
It is of the utmost importance that all workers we introduce demonstrate respect for our clients and their property and act in a safe, secure, honest and responsible way at all times. Here is a list of some dos and don'ts:

Respect for Clients
What we say in the booklet:
The following activities are STRICTLY PROHIBITED:

a) Smoking, consuming alcohol or eating whilst on client property.
b) Unauthorised use of the client's telephone, equipment or property.
c) Sub contracting your work to friends, relatives or anyone else.
We need to interview everybody who starts work with a client. Please refer any interested friends or relatives to us so we can interview them accordingly.

Why we say it:
Common sense really, but you need to say it so that you are seen to be doing your duty. There is always the potential for one 'bad apple'. Don't forget that anything stated in your information booklet becomes part of the formal agreement with the cleaner, therefore, provides grounds for termination if they do not comply.

Honesty
What we say in the booklet:
It goes without saying that the highest levels of honesty are required. This not only applies to clients money and possessions but also ensuring you only claim for the hours actually worked, particularly when the client is not present whilst you are working.

Why we say it:
Self explanatory, but you need to say it so there is no room for any misunderstanding.

Irons
What we say in the booklet:
Always ensure that irons are switched off after use and never place them flat down (even when switched off). If you feel the iron has cooled down enough still take care to position it in an upright position.

Why we say it:
Common sense really, but you need to say it so there is no room for any misunderstanding.

Cooker Hobs
What we say in the booklet:
Beware of flat-topped cooker hobs. When cleaning, it is easy to brush against a switch or knob and accidentally turn on the hob. Do not rest cloths, magazines or anything else on these hobs. Also take care not to drop anything on ceramic hobs as this may cause them to crack.

Why we say it:
Common sense really, but you need to say it so there is no room for any misunderstanding.
Gas
What we say in the booklet:
Gas hobs, cookers and fires can all be accidentally switched on or left on by someone unfamiliar with the controls in a strange house. Be extra careful when wiping or dusting the controls and take appropriate action if you smell gas.

Why we say it:
Common sense really, but you need to say it so there is no room for any misunderstanding.

Abrasive Cleaners and Smooth Surfaces
What we say in the booklet:
Beware of smooth surfaces, for example white sinks and white kitchen surfaces as these can easily mark or chip. Clients do notice these things so please be careful. NEVER use abrasive cleaners or cloths on any surfaces. Check with the client first to see what they use.

Why we say it:
To educate cleaners who are unfamiliar with the proper use of abrasives.

Taps
What we say in the booklet:
Taps can easily be left dripping and this can lead to serious flooding if the plug is left in the plughole. Be sure to turn off all taps and never leave plugs in the sink.

Why we say it:
Common sense really, but you need to say it so there is no room for any misunderstanding.

Security
What we say in the booklet:
Unless instructed otherwise by clients ALWAYS LOCK UP SECURELY WHEN YOU LEAVE – be sure to check all windows and doors.

Why we say it:
It's common sense really, but you need to say it so there is no room for any misunderstanding.

Working at Heights
What we say in the booklet:
Do not stand on chairs or other items of furniture to clean high surfaces or to reach something. We recommend that you only undertake such tasks if you are provided with a stepladder or other appropriate equipment. When working above head height always request that the client is present to provide assistance, if required.

Why we say it:
Many accidents in the home are caused by working at heights.

Working Outside
What we say in the booklet:
Our Insurance does not cover you if you have an accident whilst cleaning the **outside** of a client's house, for example cleaning the outside of windows. Politely decline such work if requested by the client unless the client's household insurance covers you for any accidents and you wish to undertake such work.

Why we say it:
Self explanatory.

First Aid Kit
What we say in the booklet:
Ask the client to show you where they keep their First Aid Kit. This is important if you have an accident.

Why we say it:
The client has a duty of care to provide a basic first aid kit. They are not expensive. If they don't already have one, just say it is always a good idea to have one on hand for them and their family.

Cleaning Products
What we say in the booklet:
Read the manufacturer's safety and instruction labels carefully and only products in the way prescribed. Know what do if you have an accident.

Why we say it:
Common sense really, but you need to say it so there is no room for any misunderstanding.

Cleaning Routines

What we say in the booklet:

1) Ask the client to list out the work to undertake on the Task List form. To assist the client in compiling their lists you may wish to ask them to consider each room at three levels:

- **Upper Level**
  For example: cobwebs, curtain rails / pelmets, door tops, ceiling lights and fitments.

- **Mid Level:**
  For example: pictures, lamps, ornaments, switches, cupboard doors, surfaces and window ledges.

- **Low / Floor Level**
  For example: carpets, wooden floors, skirting boards, rugs, under furniture and beds.

Work from the highest level down. In this way any dust / dirt will fall to the floor where it can be vacuumed.

2) For reasons of hygiene we encourage clients to use a colour coding system to prevent cross contamination. To enable you to operate this system the client should provide you with colour coded gloves and clothes. We recommend:

- Yellow for kitchen and food preparation areas.
- Red for toilets, bidets and other sanitary appliances.
- Blue for other low risk areas.

If the client does not wish to follow the colour coding system then at least ask them to supply a separate bathroom cleaning kit so that all cleaning products and equipment may be kept in one place thus eliminating the risk of cross contamination.

3) Always work from the cleanest to the dirtiest areas in the house, for example complete the kitchen before moving on to bathroom and toilets.

Why we say it:
This is a tried and trusted system that minimises the risk of cross contamination. We are coaching cleaners and clients who may have got into bad habits.

Cleaning Tips

What we say in the booklet:

Always tidy away before cleaning, for example take dirty dishes to the kitchen and put any loose toys in the toy box.

Always dust before vacuuming, as the dusting process will dislodge any particles onto the floor where they can be hovered up.

A dampened, clean cotton cloth is a very effective duster. To dampen, simply hold the cloth by one corner and lightly mist with clean water from a spray bottle. The cloth should be just damp enough to pick up dust without leaving moisture streaks.

When dusting wall units, first lift and dust any ornaments or other objects, then dust the shelf both underneath and behind. Start from the top of the unit and work your way down to the bottom.

Never dust a warm or hot light bulb with a damp cloth, as you may give yourself an electric shock or shatter the bulb.

An effective way to remove dust from awkward places (for example: louvered doors, telephone keys, carved furniture, etc.) is to use a dampened and clean, soft paintbrush.

To remove pet fur from upholstery use a damp cloth or rubber glove.

On tiled or vinyl floors, sweep or vacuum first to collect crumbs, loose hair and dirt before damp mopping. Start mopping in the farthest corner of the room and work your way toward the door.

To clean the narrow space between kitchen appliances, try using a cloth on the end of a mop or broom handle.

To loosen any baked on food in microwave cookers, place a cup of water inside and set the controls on high for a few minutes. The steam should soften up the splatters for easier removal.

Cooker burner rings and drip pans will be easier to clean if they are first soaked in a sink full of hot, soapy water to loosen the baked spills.

To maintain vacuum cleaners at maximum suction change the vacuum bag as recommended by the manufacturer. Please note that some vacuums eg. Dyson do not have bags but must be emptied when the dirt reaches the level marked on the collection chamber

Poor vacuum suction may indicate a blocked hose, which can easily be checked by disconnecting the hose at both ends and then seeing if a coin will drop through it. If the coin does not fall out there is probably a blockage, otherwise the problem lies elsewhere.

To straighten the fringe on rugs, sweep away from the centre of the rug using a plastic hairbrush.

When cleaning pictures frames, start at the top of the frame, then clean down the sides and across the bottom.

Chrome can be made to gleam by simply using a dry cloth.

Dust may be removed from the front of stereo speakers with the vacuum hose and flat attachment. Be careful to avoid damaging the delicate speaker mechanisms.

Use a power head to vacuum carpeted areas, but never use a beater bar on hard surfaces as it can cause damage.

Cleaning products may be limited to a quality window/glass cleaner, all-purpose cleaner, tile/grout cleaner and a toilet bowl cleaner.

Never mix two cleaning products together as it may cause a dangerous reaction, for example it may create dangerous fumes.

To avoid damage never put wet cloths, bottles, buckets or damp mops on furniture, carpets, hardwood floors, etc.

Check underneath furniture before hovering to prevent small items such as toys, money, jewellery, etc. being sucked up.

A good way to remove cobwebs is to tie a lightly dampened cloth round the end of a mop or broom.

To clean mini blinds close the slats and dust, then close the slats in the opposite way to dust the other side

Do not spray glass cleaner directly onto picture glass, computer monitors or TV screens. Instead spray a little glass cleaner on a cloth, as this will prevent streaks and keep the spray off areas that might be harmed by direct contact with the cleaner.

Beware when cleaning electrical equipment - always check the manufacturer's manual for instructions.

Why we say it:
These are tried and trusted tips that will assist the cleaner in her duties. We are providing guidance to cleaners who may have got into bad habits.

Client Checklist
What we say in the booklet:
This is a useful list of things to cover when you meet the client for the first time.

- Get the client to talk you through what they want done and how they would like you to do it. We have provided Task list forms to help with this.
- Identify any cherished / valuable Items that the client does not want you to clean.
- Find out where cleaning equipment is stored and how it works, for example how to empty the vacuum.
- Find out what cleaning products the client is supplying and if they want you to follow the colour coding cleaning system.
- Ask the client to complete the Cleaner Earning Receipt Record, to cover each session worked.
- Remind the client that you are paid in cash at the end of each cleaning session.
- Complete a Key Security Form if they expect you to let yourself in.
- Find out how to activate / deactivate the house security system, if one is fitted and they expect you to let yourself in.
- Find out the whereabouts of the First Aid Kit.
- Exchange telephone number information with the client. You will both need to contact one another at some point in time.
- Find out if the client has any pets and, if appropriate, agree how these will be dealt with when you call.

Why we say it:
You have given the cleaner a great deal of information to absorb so you need to help her remember the important points to cover when she starts work with the client.

Incentive Scheme
What we say in the booklet:
We operate an incentive scheme that pays a fee of £10 for each Cleaner or Client you introduce to us. Some terms and conditions apply so please ask us for further details.

Why we say it:
You always need new cleaners so this is a brilliant way to generate referrals. The terms and conditions would be that the cleaner passes your vetting procedures and stays with a client for at least 2 weeks.

Useful Financial Information

What we say in the booklet:

For financial information we recommend you visit the following website:
http://www.hmrc.gov.uk/individuals/index.shtml

Why we say it:

You have previously told the cleaner that she is responsible for her tax affairs so why not give her a bit of help by directing her to the appropriate government website.

Record of Client Contact Details:

RECORD OF CLIENT CONTACT DETAILS

This form is to record client contact details and work schedules. This is useful if you need to contact clients. For example, if you need to advise them that you cannot attend work.

Name: ____________________ Tel Eve: ____________________
Address: ____________________ Tel Day: ____________________
____________________ Business No: ____________________
____________________ Days: ____________________
________ Postcode: __________ Times: ____________________
Other Notes: ____
____
____

Name: ____________________ Tel Eve: ____________________
Address: ____________________ Tel Day: ____________________
____________________ Business No: ____________________
____________________ Days: ____________________
________ Postcode: __________ Times: ____________________
Other Notes: ____
____
____

Name: ____________________ Tel Eve: ____________________
Address: ____________________ Tel Day: ____________________
____________________ Business No: ____________________
____________________ Days: ____________________
________ Postcode: __________ Times: ____________________
Other Notes: ____
____
____

12

Why we provide it:
The last page of your Worker Information Booklet should contain a Client Contact Record which enables the cleaner to keep a proper record of her clients' contact details rather than writing them on the 'back of a cigarette packet' or something similar that could be easily lost.

Terms of Association Agreement

After you have covered the main information within the Worker handbook you should move onto your Terms of Association agreement which covers contractual matters between you and the cleaner.

As explained earlier the cleaner is not employed by you, therefore a contract of employment would be inappropriate. Instead your contractual relationship should be covered by the Terms of Association agreement which spells out the rights and obligations on both sides.

For guidance purposes only, I have provided you with a specimen agreement below. I grant you permission to use this agreement, providing you have purchased my book, but it is highly recommended that you carry out your own contract assessments with a qualified lawyer to determine appropriate terms and conditions to suit the particular requirements of your business and the current laws of the country you operate in. For these reasons I cannot provide any guarantees that specimen agreement will be suitable for your business.

Like any legal agreement it can be a bit difficult to understand as it has been written by a lawyer, so you will need to explain it in layman's terms to the cleaner. For your clarification I've included an explanation of each clause underneath the specimen agreement.

Add Your Company Details and Logo Here

TERMS OF ASSOCIATION

Add your Company Name here (The Company) provides a cleaner introduction service. Our main function is to maintain a database of carefully vetted cleaners who we place with clients requiring cleaning and ironing services. You are employed by clients of the Company who set your specific duties and pay you directly.

Please note that clients we introduce to you belong to The Company, not you.

By signing this agreement you hereby agree to the following terms of association:

1) You must not treat clients we introduce to you as your personal clients.

2) You must not at any time seek to deal directly with The Company clients.

3) You must not do anything to cause The Company to lose clients, either during your association with us or after leaving us.

4) During your association with The Company or for a period of six months after leaving The Company's database you must not directly or indirectly, without The Company's written consent:

> a) Attempt to solicit or entice away The Company's clients.
> For the sake of clarity a client of The Company shall mean a person to whom it has supplied professional services within a period of two years prior to the material date.
>
> b) Finance or otherwise be engaged or interested in any business activity competitive with all or part of the business carried out by The Company or work for any of The Company's clients, with whom you had direct contact, within a radius of ten miles from where employed.'

5) During or at any other time after termination of your association with The Company make use of any business, corporate or other name which in any way suggests a connection with The Company or any of The Company clients.

6) If The Company's fee is not paid by a client for whom you are working, we would require you to cease working for that client. In this respect there must be a degree of trust and co-operation between us. In return we will endeavour to provide you with a replacement client at the earliest opportunity.'

If any proviso of the above clauses is found to be un-enforceable it does not affect the validity of those remaining.

I have read the above terms of association and agree to abide by them together with the notes and instructions contained in the "Add your company name here Worker Information Booklet" which I have read and understood.'

Signature: .... Date: ....

Once you are satisfied that your cleaner understands the agreement ask her to sign and date it. Remember to give the cleaner a copy for her records.

Now let's look at the various clauses making up this agreement and what they mean:

'Add your Company Name here (The Company) provides a cleaner introduction service. Our main function is to maintain a database of carefully vetted cleaners who we place with clients requiring cleaning and ironing services.'

Clearly states the purpose of your business.

'You are employed by clients of the Company who set your specific duties and pay you directly.'

This reminds the cleaner that she is employed by the clients you provide and that they pay her directly.

'Please note that clients we introduce to you belong to The Company, not you.
1) You must not treat clients we introduce to you as your personal clients.
2) You must not at any time seek to deal directly with The Company clients.'

This reminds the cleaner that she should not regard your clients as being hers. This is to stop her dealing directly with your clients. For example, the client and cleaner may conspire to strike up a private arrangement by cutting you out. The sole purpose of this would be to avoid paying your services fees and should not be tolerated.

'3) You must not do anything to cause The Company to lose clients, either during your association with us or after leaving us.'

Self explanatory.

'4) During your association with The Company or for a period of six months after leaving The Company's database you must not directly or indirectly, without The Company's written consent:

> a) Attempt to solicit or entice away The Company's clients.
> For the sake of clarity a client of The Company shall mean a person to whom it has supplied professional services within a period of two years prior to the material date.'
>
> This clause is primarily aimed at preventing your cleaner from poaching your clients whilst working for your agency, or 6 months after she left.
>
> 'b) Finance or otherwise be engaged or interested in any business activity competitive with all or part of the business carried out by The Company or work for any of The Company's clients, with whom you had direct contact, within a radius of ten miles from where employed.'
>
> This is to prohibit the cleaner being involved in another cleaning business that competes with your business whilst she is working for you or for a period 6 months after she has left. It also prevents her from making contact with your clients within a 10 mile radius of where she worked for a period of 6 months after she left you. This is to stop the cleaner setting up a cleaning business with a third party and stealing your clients.

'5) During or at any other time after termination of your association with The Company make use of any business, corporate or other name which in any way suggests a connection with The Company or any of The Company clients. '

This clause is primarily there to prevent the cleaner trading under a name very similar to your company's name, with the purpose of gaining commercial advantage.

'6) If The Company's fee is not paid by a client for whom you are working, we would require you to cease working for that client. In this respect there must be a degree of trust and co-operation between us. In return we will endeavour to provide you with a replacement client at the earliest opportunity.'

This means that if a client stops paying your services fee, you have the right to withdraw the cleaner. However, if this happens you will endeavour to provide her with replacement clients at the earliest opportunity.

'If any proviso of the above clauses is found to be un-enforceable it does not affect the validity of those remaining.'

This means that in the event of the agreement being tested in court, all the clauses should be read separately. In this way if any clause is deemed to be unfair or unenforceable, the other clauses may remain in place.

'I have read the above terms of association and agree to abide by them together with the notes and instructions contained in the "Add your company name here Worker Information Booklet" which I have read and understood.'

When the cleaner signs this agreement she is not only agreeing to your terms and conditions but also the instructions provided in the Worker Information Booklet.

The Cleaner Weekly Earnings Declaration

Before your cleaner begins work with any of your clients, you must explain the importance of completing a 'Cleaner Weekly Earnings Record' which provides a summary of her total client earnings at the end of each week. You should tell the cleaner that the form is necessary as it ensures you can keep track of her hours, but stress this is an internal document which does not get sent to the 'tax man'. Why is this form important to us?

a) To ensure we can closely monitor the cleaner's total weekly earnings so they do not exceed the lower of the income tax or National Insurance thresholds (as explained earlier in the book).
b) To keep track on the number of hours taken by each client. Don't forget you are paid a services fee based on the average number of hours worked by your cleaners, therefore if a client increases the number of hours on a regular basis you will need to ask them to sign an amended Standing Order form.
c) You need to confirm that any increases in the cleaner's hourly rate are kept track of and factored in to your monitoring system.

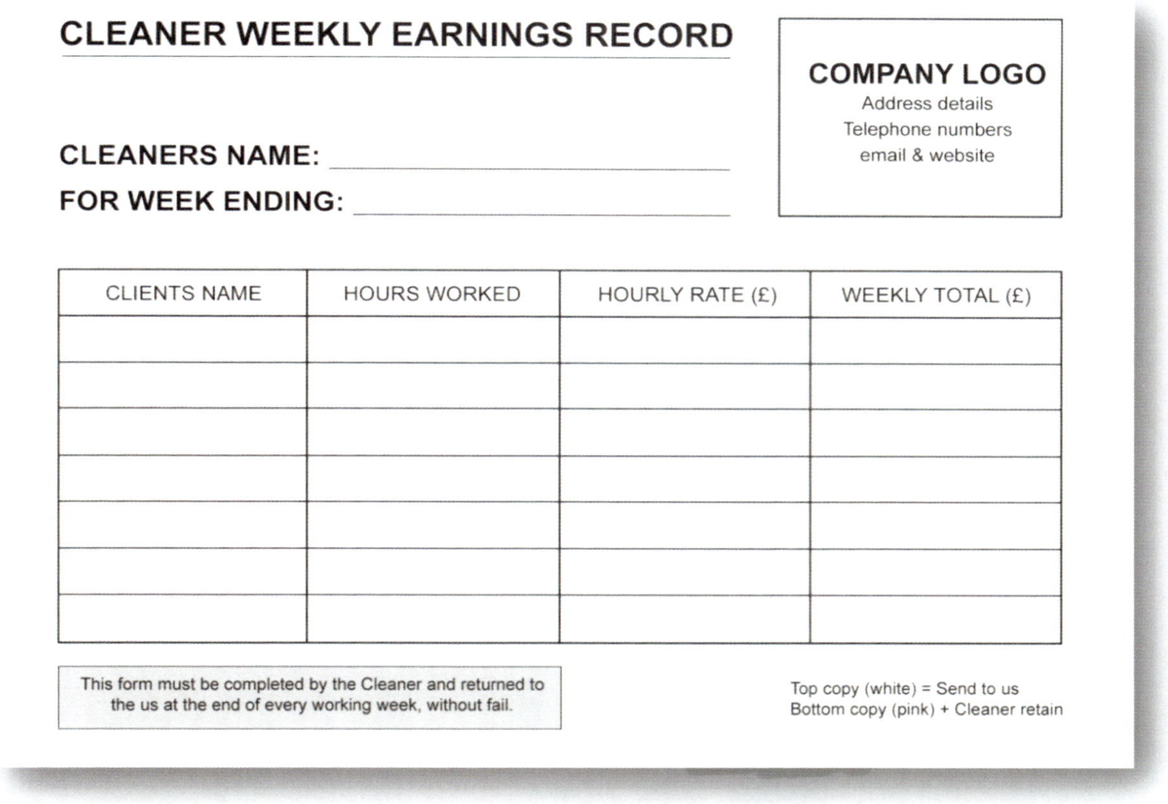

CLEANER WEEKLY EARNINGS RECORD

COMPANY LOGO
Address details
Telephone numbers
email & website

CLEANERS NAME: ____________________

FOR WEEK ENDING: ____________________

CLIENTS NAME	HOURS WORKED	HOURLY RATE (£)	WEEKLY TOTAL (£)

This form must be completed by the Cleaner and returned to the us at the end of every working week, without fail.

Top copy (white) = Send to us
Bottom copy (pink) + Cleaner retain

I would recommend you give your cleaner enough forms for 3 months and then top her up as required. You may also wish to provide your cleaners with postage paid, pre-addressed envelopes as this will make the task easier and not hit their pocket. Once you know the cleaner has got into the habit of completing the forms on a weekly basis you may wish to consider relaxing the actual return of the forms to say once a fortnight or once a month. However, I would not advocate this if the cleaner is close to her Income Tax or National Insurance thresholds as you need to make sure she doesn't exceed these.

Alternatively, you may wish to introduce an email system whereby you send the cleaner a weekly reminder and they reply to you with details of how many hours they have worked per client. You should of course file all of the emails away for tax purposes (i.e. in case you are ever audited). I would recommend you print off a hard copy which is retained for a minimum of 6 years.

Cleaner Identification Badge

The cleaner identification badge serves three purposes:

- It provides ID if called upon, for example some elderly and nervous customers may ask for identification to prove the cleaner is from your business.
- It makes you look more professional
- It makes the cleaner feel part of your organisation.

The badge is not essential but they take so little time to produce I'd recommend you consider using them. The written information on the badge can be produced in a word processing program like Microsoft Word, then you add the passport photograph already provided by the cleaner at the first interview. Finally you enclose the above in a special badge holder which you can get from any good stationers. Here's the catalogue number of a cheap badge holder provided by Staples:

Item Number: WW-372892, about £4 per 50, plus postage and packing.

It costs very little but creates a great impression.

Here is a sample layout:

EVERYTHING YOU NEED TO KNOW ABOUT CLIENTS

Identifying Client Rich Areas

I mentioned earlier that the sustained demand for domestic cleaning services in recent years is due to a number of socio-economic factors:

- Increased disposable income levels, particularly among dual-income households.
- An increase in the numbers of women employed outside the home.
- Far greater focus on leisure over domestic responsibilities (the live hard, play hard ethos).
- An increasing social acceptance of having help in the home. This is now seen as a status symbol rather than a stigma.

Based on the above profile here is a non-exhaustive list of the type of customers you will want to target to build up a successful client-base:

- **Young Professionals and Double Income Couples.**
  Today's professionals often work long and stressful hours, with little time for leisure and relaxation, leaving no desire to spend what little free time they have doing the housework. Commuter towns or residential areas close to cities are a rich source for this type of client.

- **Mums with Young Children**
  This portion of the market is large, however opportunities for custom may be harder to find as disposable income can be lower within this group. It is also worth noting that young mums will usually have a network of friends that are also young mums, so it may be possible to boost your reputation and gain promotion through word of mouth.

- **Senior Citizens and Disabled People**
  For obvious reasons this demographic may find it difficult to carry out the cleaning on their entire property, so need a helping hand with some of the more arduous tasks. Many older clients also like to have a cleaner because it provides them with a bit of company.

- **Single Men**
  Notoriously uninterested in the cleaning process, single men are a good source of clients.

- **Privileged Individuals or Families**
  Usually living in affluent areas, this group has larger than average disposable income and are the kind of people that would admit they enjoy being pampered. They are normally highly sociable people, which is beneficial in spreading your reputation.

- **People Moving House**
  A lucrative sideline to regular cleaning work are houses requiring one off cleans.
  Typically tenants of rented property require this service at the end of the rental period in order to secure the return of deposit monies held by estate agents.

You need to get a picture in your head of these main customer groups so that as you drive around in your car you can start to consider areas you want to target.

I would recommend buying a map of your target town which you can colour code to indicate potential client areas and potential cleaner areas.

Clients are more likely to be found in the nicer private houses and apartments. You can also look for other factors like being near to a railway station, a hospital (for medical professionals) or in retirement properties.

Cleaners are more likely to be found in council or housing association properties.

The ideal socio-economic mix would be where client and cleaner areas are closely located, as cleaners do not like to travel long distances to work because of transport costs eating away at their relatively small hourly rate.

Finding and Converting Clients

There are a number of tried and tested ways of finding clients. Here are some methods I would recommend:

Local Newspaper Advertising

We looked at local newspaper advertising as a means to recruit cleaners, so you should have already a put together a list serving your targeted area. Now go to the Trades & Services section and take down the details of who to call if you want to place an advertisement.

Newspaper	Telephone	Contact Name	Distribution	Circulation	Rate	Comments

When you call them you need to explain that you are just setting up a business and need some information. You need to find out the following:

- **The Distribution**
  You should already have this information from when you called about placing a cleaner recruitment advertisement.

- **The Circulation**
  You should already have this information from when you called about placing a cleaner recruitment advertisement.

- **The Advertising Rates**
  Ask the sales team to send you a 'rate card' which will detail out the cost of advertising per newspaper title under their control. Bigger publishers may offer a reduced rate for advertising in more than one title in their stable.

  Top Tips:

  I. ***As with all advertising, you need to be able to pick out what works and what doesn't so when clients call you must try to find out where they saw your ad.***
  II. ***Drop any newspaper media that is not working for you.***
  III. ***Ask for discount if you commit to advertise for a longer period.***
  IV. ***Ask if the newspaper will run your press release for free if you advertise with them.***
  V. ***Find out the deadline for advertising copy. If you call them near to that time they will often slash rates if they have space to fill.***

Client Promotional Cards (via letterbox drops)

Direct marketing still works! My recommendation is that you use postcard size (A6 size) promotional material instead of leaflets as in my experience you tend to get a better response. Cards are easier to file away and are more durable than leaflets. I've known customers to contact us several months after the postcard has been dropped with them.

Promotional material needs to do three things: *grab* the audience's attention, *convince* them that your service is perfect for them, and then cause them to *act* on it.

Here are some good guidelines to follow to create a great promotional card that converts:

1) Make It Professional

The first mistake any new business can make is to reduce its marketing spend. Distributing promotional cards which are poorly designed and cheaply-made can make your business look amateurish and that is the last message you wish to convey. So when you produce your client cards, I recommend you make them professional and impressive or it could lead to a poor response.

2) An Attention Grabbing Headline

There's a brutal test for how successful your headline is: you've got the time from when your customer picks up your promotional card to when they reach for their waste bin. If your headline can catch their attention in those fifteen seconds, then you will have a much better chance of converting them. Try something like 'Do You Hate Housework?'

3) Avoid Long Sentences

You only have a small amount of time to convince your reader, so keep your sentences snappy and don't wear out their attention spans. Bullet points can be an excellent way to cover a lot of ground quickly.

4) Sell the Benefits, Not the Features

Often we see promotional material that goes into great detail about the features of a cleaning service, but completely ignore the benefits. You may offer an excellent maid finding service but your client wants to know that it will save her time, make her life easier, give her more leisure time etc.

5) Include 'Power Phrases'

Grab your audience's attention and keep them interested with active, exciting power phrases like 'Enjoy more precious leisure time' or 'Get your life back' etc.

6) A Picture's Worth a Thousand Words

Images are a great way to capture the attention of your readers faster than words can. Keep it relevant, exciting & even humorous and it will stay in your client's mind long after they've put down your card.

7) Avoid Clutter

Don't put too much information on your client cards, it will intimidate your audience and make them feel like it isn't worth the bother. Leaving blank spaces will encourage your readers that your promotional message won't be much effort to read.

8) Don't Forget The Detail

Believe it or not, we've known companies to print 100,000 flyers only to find they've left off crucial information like their telephone number! Now that really is a soft sell!

9**) Call to Action**

Make sure you end by telling your audience what to do next. It can be as simple as 'Call 01234 567890' or 'To End Your Housework Blues for Good Please Call 01234 567890'

You may wish to consider incentivising your customer to use your company immediately. If they think there's a discount or a special gift for a limited period they'll be less likely to put off their decision. For example 'Call Today and We'll Give You Our Free Book On ....' or 'Call Today and Well Give You 50% Discount On Your First Month's Fees'

Stick to the above guidelines and you won't go far wrong, but remember to record how many responses you get from your campaign. If you are disappointed with the level of response you may need to re-evaluate and tweak your design.

Depending on the level of competition in your chosen area and the quality of your card, you should get 1 response for every 200 to 400 postcards delivered. Let's assume you deliver 10,000 cards by hand, it should generate about 30 client enquiries on average. Not bad when a typical client will bring you in about £400 per year in fees!

When I first started out my family and I personally delivered our promotional cards, but after a while you won't have time to do this so either use a reliable distribution company or find a trustworthy part time leaflet deliverer.

Here are some sample promotional cards we have used:

Sample 1 - 'Do You Hate Housework?'

Do You Hate Housework?

- Are you bogged down with cleaning and ironing?
- Are you struggling to find enough spare time?
- Has your work / life balance become one-sided?

We Can Help

Your own carefully vetted cleaner	✓	Same dedicated staff each week	✓
Pricing from only £10.50 per hr.	✓	Holiday & sickness cover provided	✓
Insurance cover included	✓	Reliable and customer focused	✓

To let us give you back your precious leisure time.

Call us today 01234 567890

Sample 2 - 'Banish Housework Forever!'

Banish Housework Forever!

- Are you bogged down with cleaning and ironing?
- Are you struggling to find enough spare time?
- Has your work / life balance become one-sided?

We Can Help

Your own carefully vetted cleaner	✓	Same dedicated staff each week	✓
Pricing from only £10.50 per hr.	✓	Holiday & sickness cover provided	✓
Insurance cover included	✓	Reliable and customer focused	✓

To let us give you back your precious leisure time.

Call us today 01234 567890

Sample 3 - Using humour (printed both sides)

As you deliver the cards make sure to keep a record of when and which streets you have delivered to. I also recommend that you show the number of clients secured in each street as this will inform you if it's worthwhile stepping up or reducing your efforts nearby. You should aim to drop the cards in your target area at least twice a year as this reinforces your original message in the mind of the householder.

Client Marketing - Drop Report

Street Name / Town	1st drop date	2nd drop date	3rd drop date	Clients secured?

I would recommend you put your information into a spreadsheet as this will make it much easier to update and review the data.

Developing an Online Presence

Nowadays having an online presence is very important as an increasing number of people are using the internet as their first port of call when trying to find local businesses. If you need proof of this just look at the size of Yellow Pages nowadays and the number of local newspapers that are struggling to survive. Here are the methods we would recommend:

- **Your Own Website**
  We can build you a customised website based on our speciality cleaning agency website template. For more information please visit:
  http://howtostartacleaningbusiness.org.uk/subsidised-website/

- **Google Places**

  Google Places is a brilliant way to promote your business on Google and best of all it is currently free to register and display your business. More information on how to get your company listed can be found at http://www.google.com/places/
  If you feel uncomfortable doing this we can do it for you for £49 plus VAT.

- **Online Directories**

  Online directories can be a great way to get your promotional message across to lots of people. One of the bonuses of buying my book is that we have negotiated a half price advertising deal in one of the UK's top on-line cleaning directories: http://www.cleaningdirectory.co.uk. The normal cost for 12 months advertising is £99 plus VAT, but you get it for just £49 plus VAT. To take advantage of this offer you simply have to email info@cleaningdirectory.co.uk quoting discount reference: *GOLDMINE 50.*

- **Google Adwords**

  This is another service offered by Google, where you can place your advertisement at the side or the top of their pages whenever anybody searches for your nominated keyword phrase(s). For example, you might decide that 'domestic cleaning Crawley' is a good keyword phrase for your business. If anybody clicks on your advertisement you pay Google an amount of money determined by how competitive your keyword is. Many companies now use this service so the cost per click may be expensive in relation to the number of enquiries you receive. For more information on Adwords I recommend you visit: http://www.google.co.uk/adwords/express/

- **Facebook Business Page**

  Create your own Facebook fan page dedicated to promoting your company. It's free and many large corporations use this resource. More information can be found here: http://www.facebook.com/about/pages.

  Below you can find some examples of Google Places, Online Directories and Google Adwords ads. appearing on a the first page of the search results for the search term 'domestic cleaning ascot':

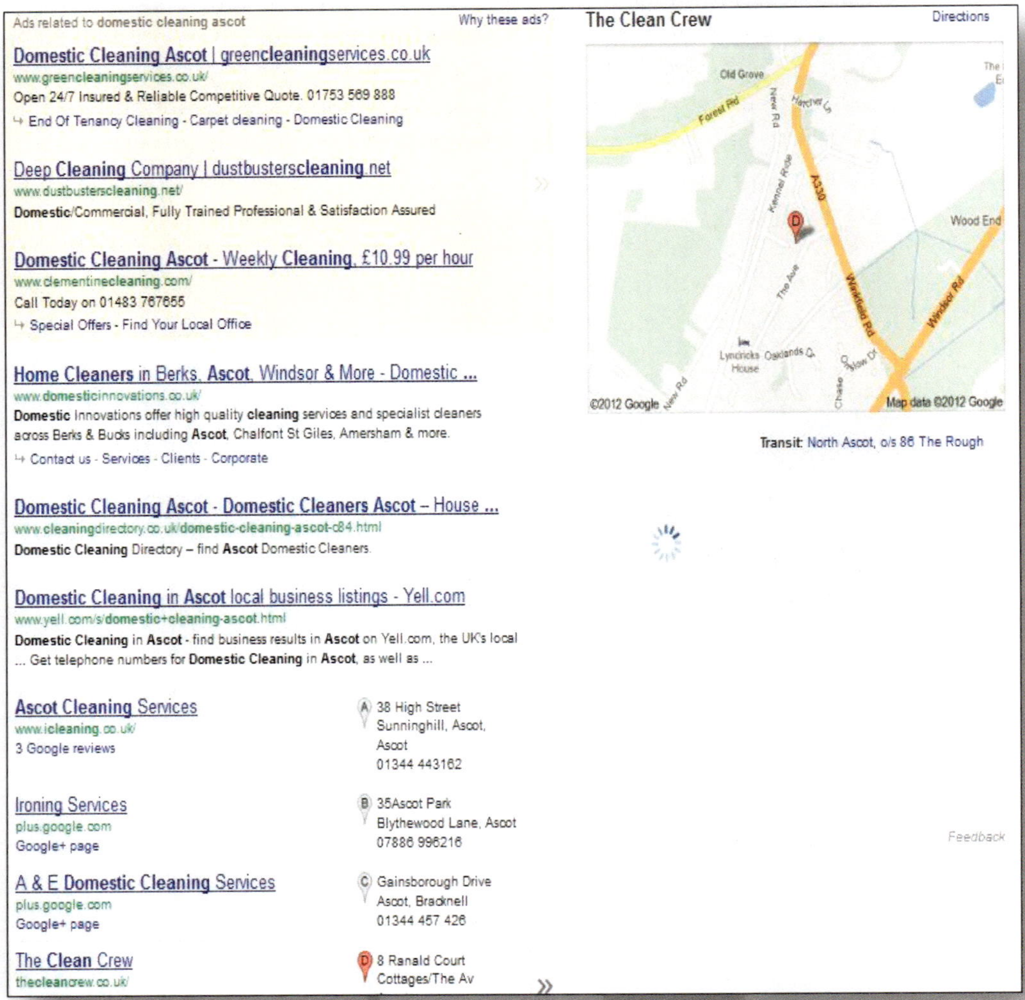

Let's analyse the above search results:

- The first 3 results are paid Google Adwords advertisements. Google Adwords pretty well guarantees you high placement in the search results but it costs you money every time someone clicks on your ad. Please note that your ads may appear on the right hand side rather than the top.
- The fourth search result is a private website. This is the best way to generate traffic to your website, as it's free.
- The fifth and sixth advertisements are online directories.
- The last 4 results are free Google Places advertisements. This requires you to register your company with Google places. We explain how to do this in this book.

Press Releases

Local newspapers are often looking for copy to fill their pages and will sometimes allow you to carry a free or reduced priced press release if you are buying advertising space from them.

Top Tip: For ideas on generating your own press release just type 'cleaning press releases' into Google search.

Client Referrals

As you get more clients they will start to recommend you. People naturally like to tell their friends and family what is happening in their lives especially when your cleaner is taking a lot of weight off their shoulders.

Top Tip: Consider offering clients an incentive if their recommendation leads to you winning a new client. For example give them Marks & Spencer's vouchers.

Village, Parish, Church Magazines

This can be an inexpensive way to generate new customers.

Local Clubs and Groups

If you think there are local clubs or groups that may contain potential clients then ask them if you may display your promotional card on their notice board.
Here are some examples: Tennis, Cricket, Rugby, Bowls, Amateur Dramatics.

Nursery and Pre-School Groups

Affluent mums often need help with housework. Ask if you can put your promotional card on their notice board. At the same time add your cleaner wanted cards.

Free Yellow Pages Listing

Contact Yellow Pages and get your business listed on their website for free. Just be aware that once they've got your details they will try to persuade you to pay for 'bigger and better' listings. You do know how to say 'No', don't you? Seriously, when you have sufficient funds you could consider what they have on offer but when money is tight the free ad is a no brainer.

Estate Agent Referrals (for end of tenancy cleans)

After you have a good number of cleaners registered with your business, you are likely to have spare capacity to deal with lucrative end of tenancy cleans.

Tenants need to do a thorough spring clean when they move out of rented accommodation or else they won't get their deposit back from the estate agent or landlord.

Often they can't face doing this because they are housework averse or don't have the time. An excellent source of referrals for this type of work is the estate agent themselves but be aware that they may require a 'commission' for doing this. Well we all know about Estate Agents!

Dealing With Client Enquiries

Okay, you've put your marketing plans into action and now you must make the most of all the potential client telephone enquiries you receive. Just as we have a cleaner contact form / script I would also recommend you develop a Client Enquiry Form which serves 2 main purposes:

I. It provides a permanent record of potential clients and when you are going to meet them.
II. It provides a script to keep you on track in terms of covering everything and controlling the conversation.

When talking with clients your tone should be confident, enthusiastic and friendly. When falling back on the script try not to read it out word for word as this will come across to the client. I like to think that every time a potential client rings I broadly sing the same tune but use slightly different lyrics. Any way before I get into karaoke analogies let's move on!

First of all deal with the client's initial enquiry then try to get some details from them. Don't feel you have to cover all the script, rather see it as a menu you can dip into to sell your services. Obviously as you become more experienced you will have less reliance on a script but when you're first starting out it is a nice 'comfort blanket' by your side. Some clients will be in a hurry and only want the bare minimum details, whereas others will want to know the 'ins and outs' of your service. After a few calls you'll soon learn to distinguish with Mrs 'Rushed' from Mrs 'Thorough', but your aim should be to sell your services and get an appointment. Even if you only manage to get their contact telephone number it will give you an opportunity to contact them at a later date.

Top Tip: Try to close the conversation with an assumption that they want to have a meeting. For example: 'When would be a good time to meet' rather than 'would you like to meet'.

As your business grows so will your confidence in dealing with clients. Until then you'll have to 'fake it until you make it' as they say. The Client Enquiry will really help with this.

You may feel more comfortable coming up with your own script and form but meantime here's one you can use.

CLIENT ENQUIRY FORM **Date:** ____________________

Good morning, (say your company name). Listen to their enquiry and than say:

Could I please take a few contact details:

Name:	Mrs / Miss / Mr :
Tel Nos:	Landline: Mobile:
Email:	
Address:	
	Post Code:

Do you require general cleaning or ironing as well? **CLEANING ONLY / CLEANING & IRONING**

How many hours do you think you will need per week?

That's all I need to for now, so let me tell you a little about us and how we work:

1. We are a family run, Cleaner Introduction Service.
2. We maintain a database of carefully vetted cleaners who are looking for work in private homes. This is a time consuming process, but is essential to safeguard client interests.

How We Vet (Use if Necessary).

a First of all we carry out a telephone screening interview designed to eliminate unsuitable applicants.

b. We then arrange to interview cleaners in their own homes. This is important as we can see how they maintain their own houses.

c. We obtain and check out 2 references from previous employers or character references.

d. We also confirm the cleaner's ID and place of abode.

e If appropriate, we also check their right to work in this country (i.e. visa and work permit).

f Finally we put all our cleaners through an induction course. *This covers cleaning procedures, health and safety, hygiene and security issues.*

g. Only when we are **fully satisfied with all aspects** of the vetting process, do we ask them to attend an interview with potential clients.

h. The bottom line is we do not allow anyone on to our books who we would not be happy to use in our own home. This means that 90% of applicants are rejected.

3. After you have taken on a cleaner we continue to provide cover if she is absent or leaves.
4. We also provide public liability insurance cover for property or personal accidents caused by the negligence of the cleaner. *It's a 'safety net' really in case you are not covered by your own insurance.*
5. The total cost of our service ranges from £x to £y per hour, (insert the appropriate figures for your agency) depending upon the number of hours you require. (Refer to hourly schedule if necessary). The more hours you take, the cheaper it gets per hour.
6. That covers the main points of our service - do you have any questions you'd like me to answer? *Answer and questions then move onto the close.*
7. OK, can we agree a suitable time to meet up to assess your requirements?
8. Thank you. I look forward to seeing you on ________________ at ____________________ Goodbye and thanks for calling.

COMMENTS / ACTION REQUIRED:

Presenting Your Services To Potential Clients

Okay, you've got an appointment with a client, now you must do your best to win their trust that your company is going to do a great job. Before you go into any meeting with a client you must be prepared, organised and motivated.

One thing that used to motivate me was the thought that each meeting I attended could generate an ongoing £400 per year (the average client value). Imagine somebody said to you 'I'm going to give you £400 each year if you can make me a decent fruit cake', you'd make the best and most delicious cake you could possibly imagine, wouldn't you? I bet you'd research all the top recipes, buy the best ingredients and carry out trial bakes until you hit upon the ultimate concoction.

Making a client presentation is no less important because you don't get a second chance of making a good first impression. If you're the type of person who is motivated by the thought of punishment or fear of failure just think about how many promotional cards you would need to deliver to get the chance of another client meeting. Ouch! - all that pavement pounding is hard on the feet!

The point I'm trying to get over is that you must find something to motivate you when making client presentations or you'll miss out. Once you're in the swing of doing them you should be converting at least 80%. In other words for every 10 presentations you make, you'll end up with 8 clients. If you are falling short of this figure you need to look at what you're saying and how you're saying it.

Don't worry I'm going to give you a sample presentation to keep you on track. If you're the type of person who feels more comfortable with informal presentations that fine, but at least have some sort of checklist of things to cover with the client so you properly explain the benefits of your service and come away with **a signed client agreement and standing order mandate**.

I remember my first client presentation - I thought I was prepared but looking back I think my performance was only worth about 3 out of 10. The client actually signed up with me anyway, but I think it was more out of pity than anything else! I came away and decided I needed to make my next presentation idiot proof so I developed a structured Power Point presentation. That's the sort of person I am; I hate flying by the seat of my pants because I'm not a natural salesperson.

Anyway here's a sample presentation I've put together for you; obviously feel free to change it to suit your style and the way you run your particular business. You will note that the presentation closely follows the contents of the Client Booklet so please refer to the appropriate sections as you go through if you need further guidance.

In fact another way of delivering a less formal presentation would be to use the Client Booklet as your checklist to keep you 'on script'.

I would recommend you start your presentation with a quick overview of your service. This is where you get the opportunity to be passionate about your business and how you are going to deliver a brilliant service for your clients.

However, if you've just started up you will also have to be realistic and tell the clients that it may take a couple of weeks to find someone because you will be recruiting specifically for them.

Obviously as your business grows the content of some slides will need updating, for example in a year's time you might be saying you have over a 100 clients and 50 vetted cleaners on your books.

This is where you get a chance to agitate the client's problem. What do I mean by that? Well you are in the business of solving housework problems and giving them more free time, so you want the client to relive the feeling of having to tackle all that horrible housework when that get home, when they would rather be sat in the garden or read a book etc.

Ask them why they need your service and they'll tell you in no uncertain terms how they're fed up with not having enough free time or they hate housework. The more they talk about this the better, you want them to feel emotionally attached to this ongoing problem that they have, because later on it will make it a lot easier to sign them up.

Sometimes I'll start by asking if they've had a cleaner before. If they have tried to recruit a cleaner themselves the chances are they may have been let down because they didn't know how to conduct the recruitment process.

Alternatively they may have been let down by one of your competitors. Either way you can portray yourself as the professional company who is going to manage this problem for your client.

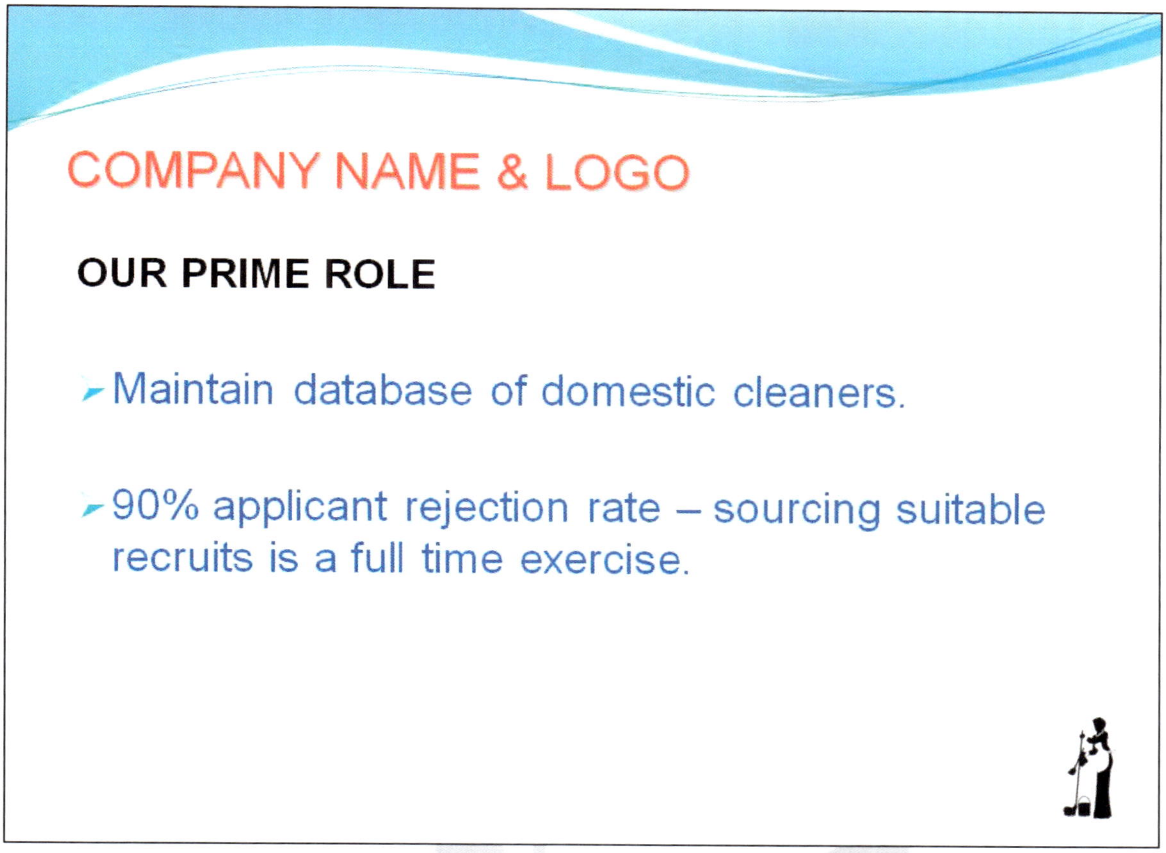

Your client may have the pre-conceived idea that what you do is simple. Let's face it the concept is dead simple, but that doesn't mean it's easy. Make sure they know that 90% of applicants don't make it onto your database register because you filter out unsuitable candidates through your thorough vetting processes.

This makes the client feel that they are in good hands and infers that if they were to recruit their own cleaner they could have a 90% chance of choosing the wrong candidate!

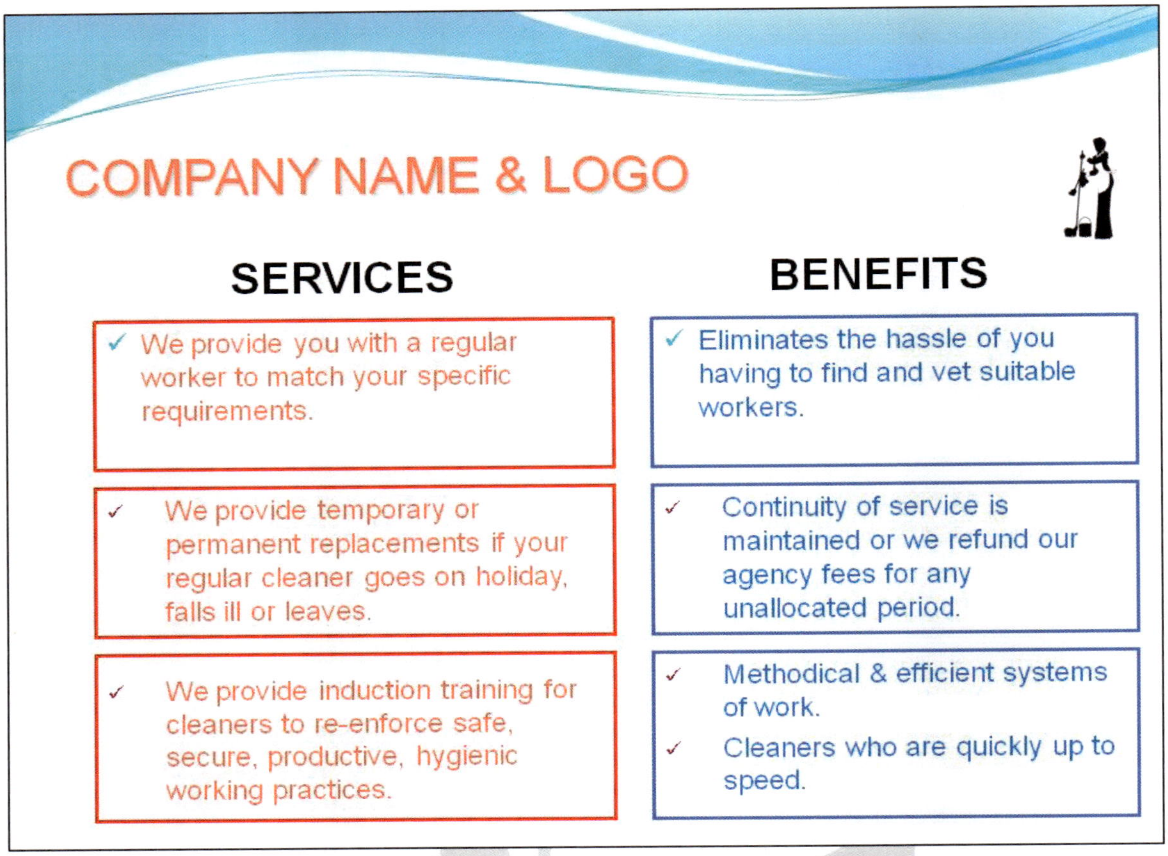

Now tell the client the services you offer and crucially the benefits they will enjoy because of your unique approach. I can tell you that 90% of your competition will explain the service they offer but not the benefits.

Clients buy when they understand the benefits of your service - don't assume they will work it out.

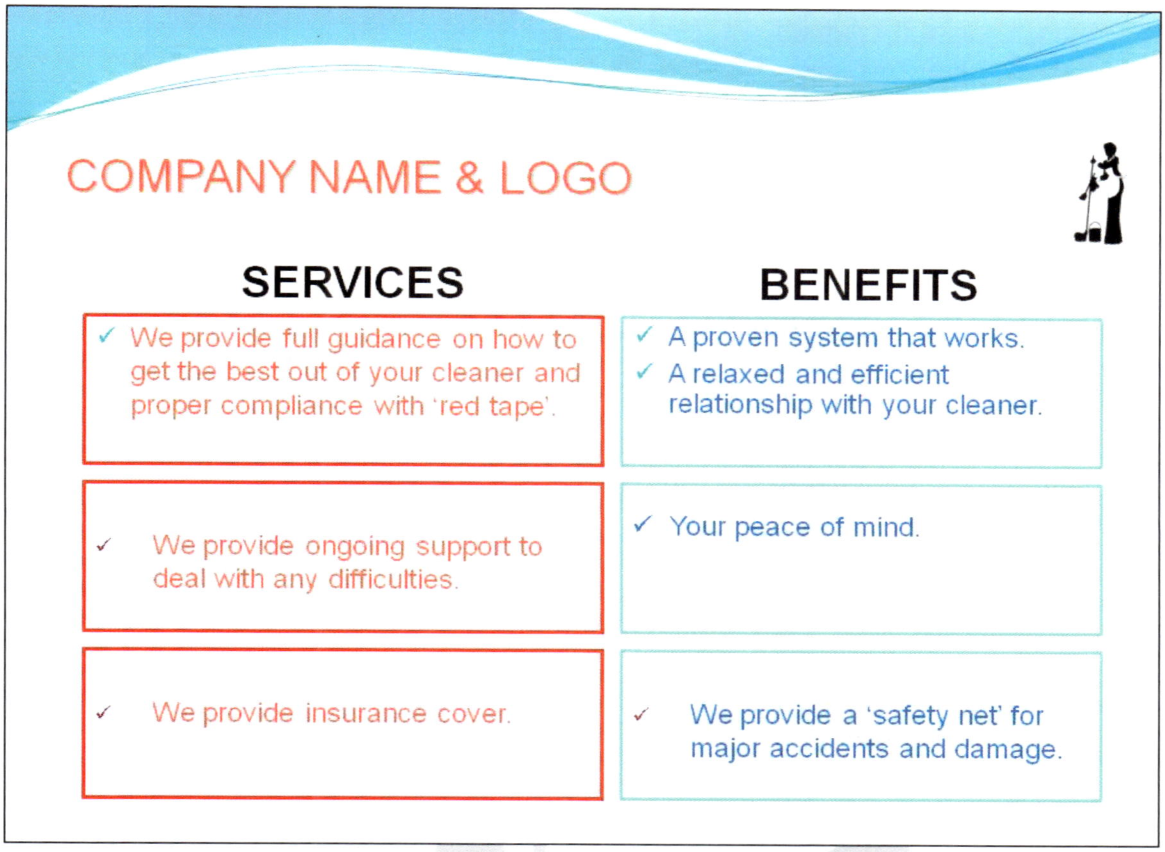

Continue to sell the benefits. Don't just read the slides out - give examples and put things in your own language.

Explain how you painstakingly find and vet your cleaners. This not only gives your clients confidence but makes them realise that you earn your fees.

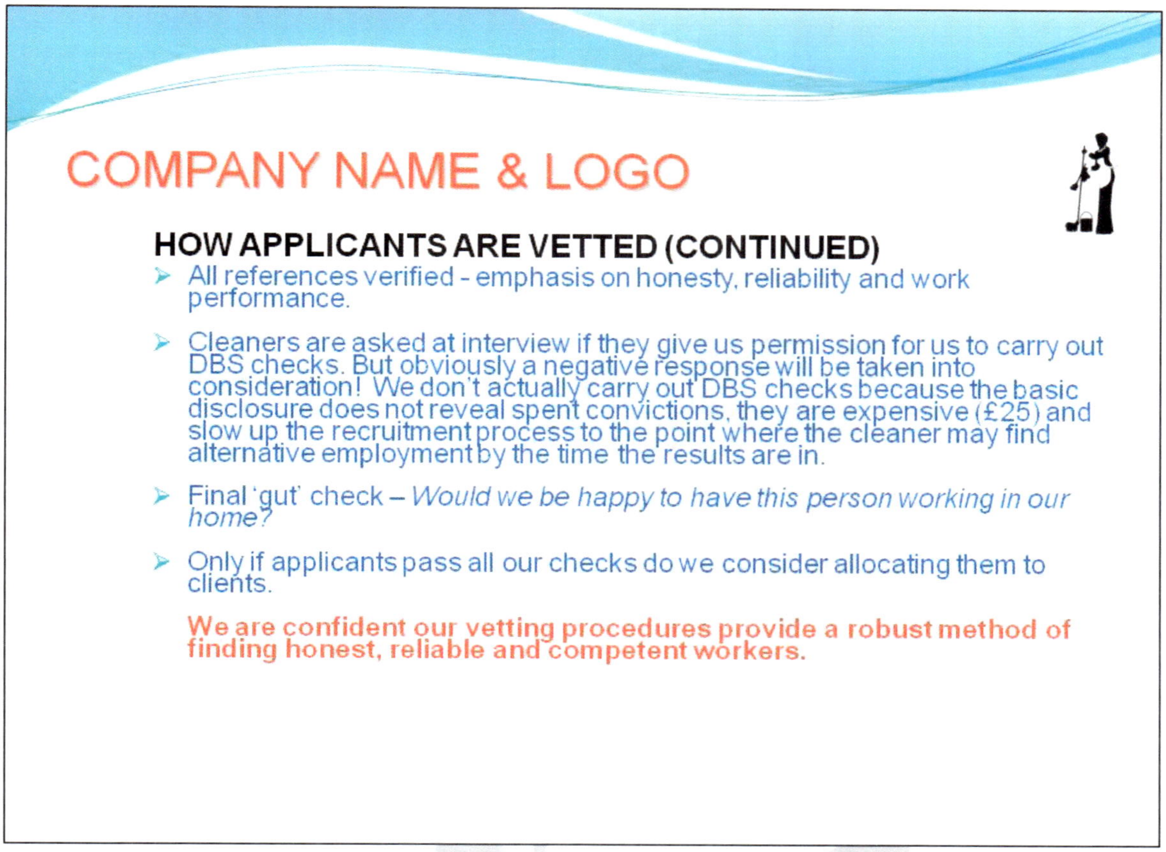

Continue to explain your vetting process. If the client is insistent on wanting a DBS Disclosure and Barring Service check it will cost £25 for a basic disclosure. DBS checks replaced the old CRB Checks in 2012. Please note that basic DBS disclosures do not reveal spent convictions.

You can get DBS checks from http://www.disclosurescotland.co.uk/basicdisclosureonline/index.htm

Should you go ahead with this I recommend you get the cleaner to apply on the basis that she is self employed and needs the information to show vulnerable clients. For example elderly, infirmed and families with young children. I also recommend you get the client to fund this as most cleaners will not be willing to bear the cost.

Sometimes you will get cleaners registering with you who are DBS checked but that is because they may have needed clearance for a previous job, like working with children. However, you cannot promise the cleaners you supply will be DBS checked.

Your client will be expecting to sign a contract so explain in simple terms how your agreement operates.

When you get to fees I like to use the analogy of a Gym where services are charged for in advance and made available to clients as and when they required. Some customers will use the Gym a lot where as others will only use it infrequently, but they still pay the same amount. It's the same with your service; sometimes clients will be unlucky and require many cleaners, whereas others may find a perfect cleaner straight away and stick with them for years.

The 'stay-ability' of cleaners is not something we can judge at interview; it is more to do with the cleaner's motivation and how well they gel with their clients. You need to be honest with your clients about that, but reassure them that there will always be a conveyor belt of vetted cleaners that you will provide to cover cleaners leaving on a permanent or temporary (holiday, sickness) basis. You are in the business of finding and vetting cleaners and that is how you earn our fees.

At this stage, if you haven't already done so, you might want to introduce the client to your Schedule of Charges which you drew up during the market research phase. You should also try to provide guidance on how many hours a client needs if they want a thorough clean of their whole house, but at the end of the day the number of hours they take will really be down to their budget. In general terms I would recommend that you work on the following guidelines:

Property Size	Minimum Number of Hours for complete house clean.
1 bedroom	2 to 2.5
2 bedroom	2.5 to 3
3 bedroom	3 to 4
4 bedroom	3.5 to 4
5 bedroom	5 to 6

Obviously each property is different so it needs to be judged individually based on the amount of clutter, number of ornaments and general state of cleanliness to begin with. If they want ironing services you will also need to add an appropriate amount of time for this.

If the client only wants 2 hours in a 4 bedroom cluttered house I would be honest with them and say that if they want a full top to bottom clean you would assess that they need about 4 hours, however, I would advise them to prioritise the work so that the most important areas are tackled first in case the cleaner runs out of time.

You should always encourage the client to take extra hours, if appropriate, but not at the risk of losing the them.

Top Tip: If you succeed in persuading a client to just take an extra 1/2 an hour per week it could generate an extra £65 per year in fees, which doesn't sound a lot in its own right but imagine 200 clients taking that extra 1/2 hour and it would amount to another £13,000 per year profit!

At this stage I normally ask the client how it all sounds so far. This serves two main purposes:

1) Psychologically this is a clever ploy because you are really asking permission to continue which is subtle way of moving her closer to using your services.

2) It teases out any initial objections which may be forming in her mind.

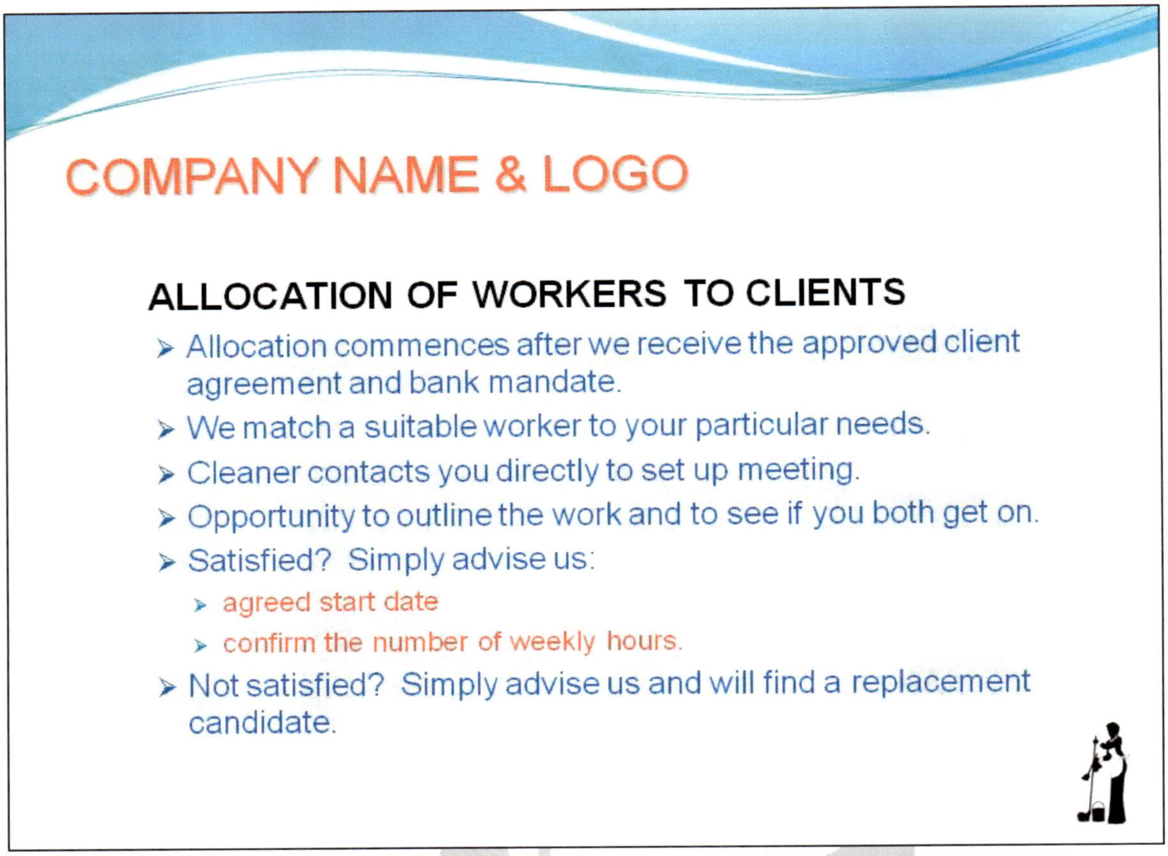

After receiving the client's permission to continue you'll move on to explain how the allocation system works and stress that you will not send the client's standing order mandate to the bank until they have interviewed the first cleaner.

The purpose of this slide is to portray an organised and professional business that has thought of everything and provides guidelines for safe systems of work and responsibilities. Talk the client through the topics highlighted above and refer them to the appropriate forms (Task List and Key Security Deposit). The client handbook covers each of these in some detail.

One area where your service saves money against some of your competitors is on cleaning equipment and products. This could be regarded as a negative factor because it could be regarded as a hidden cost; however, I try to turn it into a positive aspect.

You could say something like 'One of the things that clients like about our service is that they provide cleaners with their chosen cleaning equipment and products; that way you know it is suitable for your particular furniture and possessions. Also it prevents cross contamination caused by cleaning companies using the same equipment in their clients' houses'.

For example they may have just hovered up pet hairs. See how you've just turned a possible negative into a positive feature! That's what you should try to do with any potential objection.

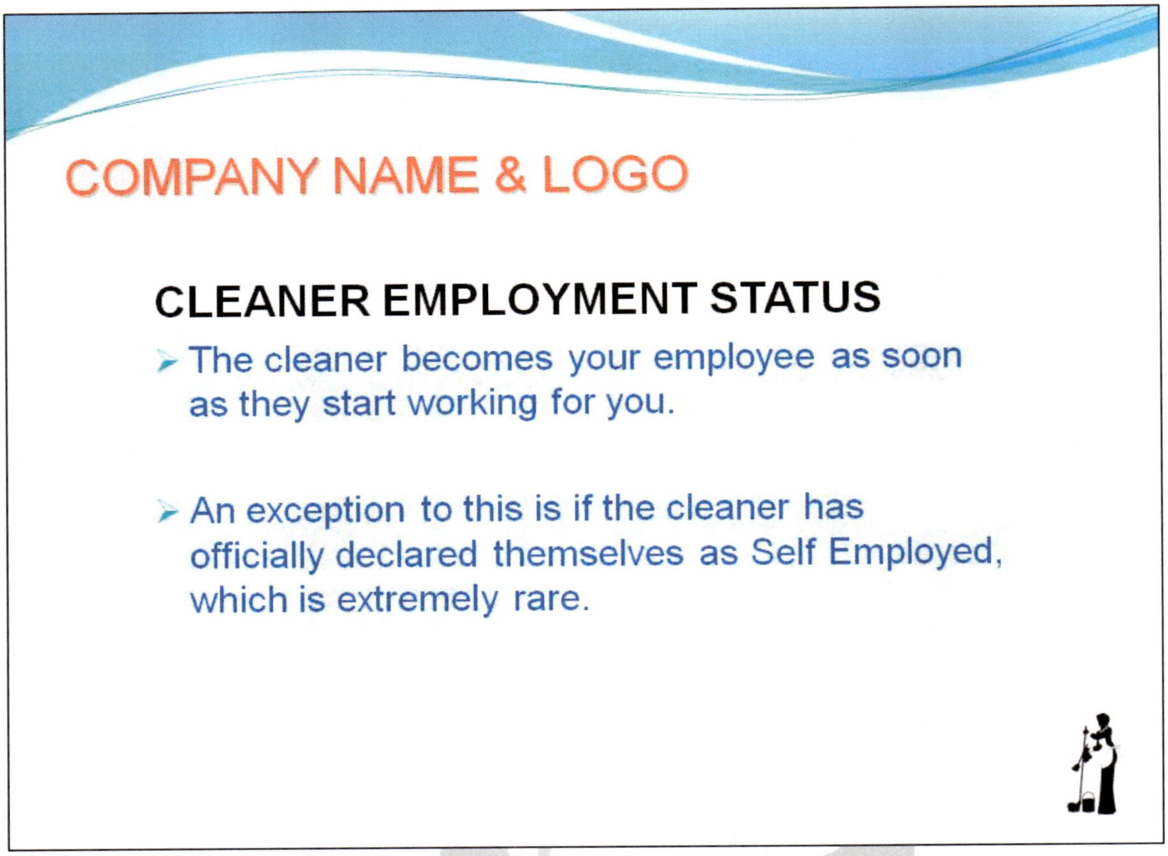

It's important that your client knows the cleaner you provide is their employee under the law.

In the previous slide you told the client that they are officially the cleaner's employer. Now you must alleviate any concerns they may have. I usually start by explaining the typical profile of a cleaner i.e. they are only looking to work restricted part time hours (usually 10 or less) to provide a little bit of extra income.

I also explain that some are on state benefits like Family Credit and would not want their part time earnings to jeopardise any benefits. This means that the chances of a cleaner earning more than the above financial limits are rare, but we have put a system in place to make sure things are monitored properly.

I explain that cleaners have to sign a declaration when they register with us which confirms they have no other jobs and have not earned more than the income tax limit in the current financial year. I then tell the client that every cleaner must submit a weekly report confirming their cumulative earnings which we log and monitor on an ongoing basis.

Finally I deal with:

- The entitlement of part time workers to receive holiday pay on a pro-rata basis. I offer to compute this for the client, if required. This is covered earlier in the book.
- How sickness and maternity pay is **not** payable because the cleaner earns below the NI lower earnings limit.

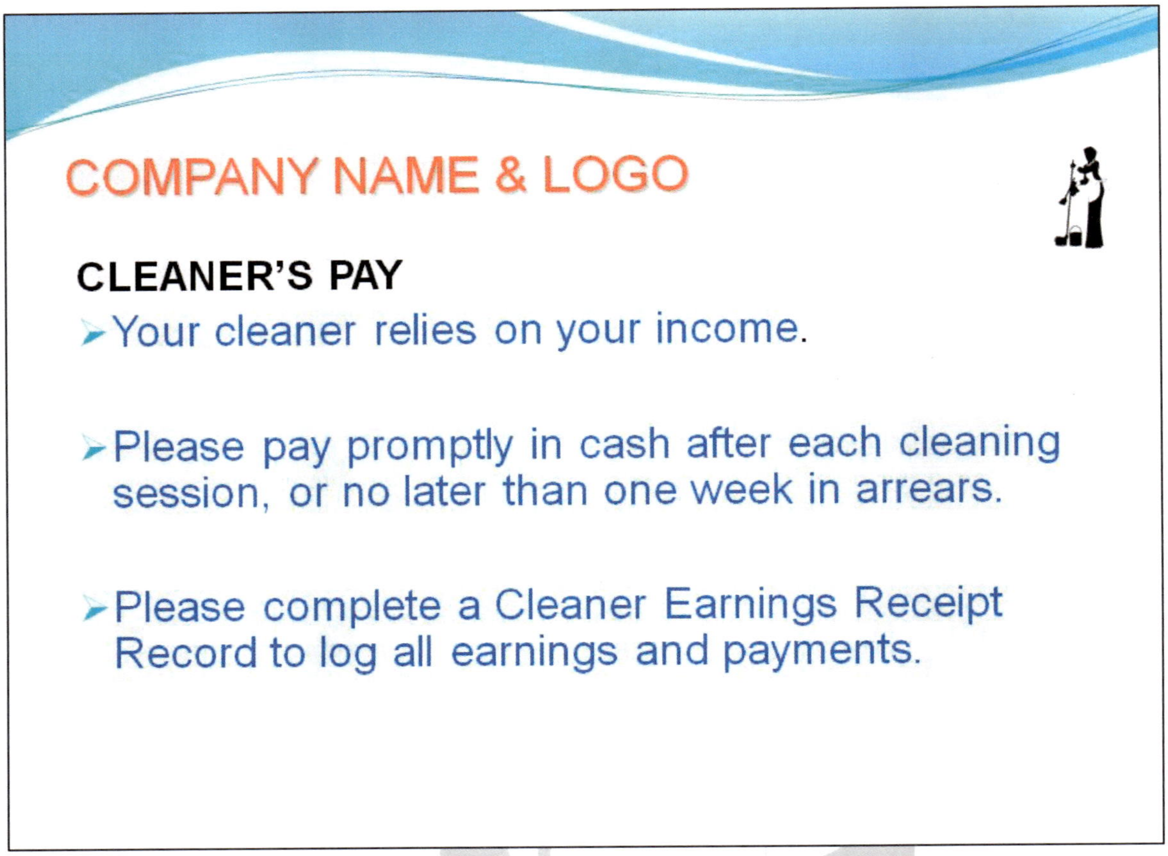

It is important your clients know that they must pay their cleaners on time, because they rely on it. Sometimes this may be for basic necessities like food or paying bills. Your clients are generally affluent so should not expect cleaners to wait for their money.

Next you need to instruct the client of the importance of the Cleaner Earnings Receipt Record, which not only confirms payment but records the number of hours worked. Advise your client that this form should be retained for 6 years for tax purposes.

Also advise them that they should send a copy of the form to us if they wish to claim a refund for any unallocated cleaner weeks.

COMPANY NAME & LOGO

INSURANCES

- We operate a public liability insurance policy providing the following cover:
  - **£xxxxxxx per claim.**
    Covers personnel injury and damage or loss of property caused by the negligence or omission of the cleaner.
- Cover only operates if your fee payment is up to date.
- Provides cover for major damage or disasters.
- Not intended to cover minor accidents and low value breakages.
- The policy has an excess of £xxx, therefore, claims under £x, are excluded.
- Clients are liable to pay the first £xxx of each claim, but your own policy may have a lower excess limit.
- Theft of belongings not covered under our insurances.
- Working outside and accidents involving bleach are excluded.

Whilst you provide public liability insurance as a benefit to clients, it is really only there for major events, not small value breakages. Explain this to the client and suggest they check their own house insurance policy to make sure it covers employer's liability to domestic workers.

This is in case the cleaner is killed or injured due to the negligence of the client. You can offer to check the policy for them if you wish and point out the appropriate clause.

Please note that some insurance brokers / insurance companies exclude the use of bleach from the cover provided in their public liability insurance policies. If this is the case you should say so in your client agreement and make this clear in the Client and Cleaner Information booklets and the above slide.

You want as much feedback as you can from your client so encourage them to call whenever they have problems or want to change the cleaner's hours.

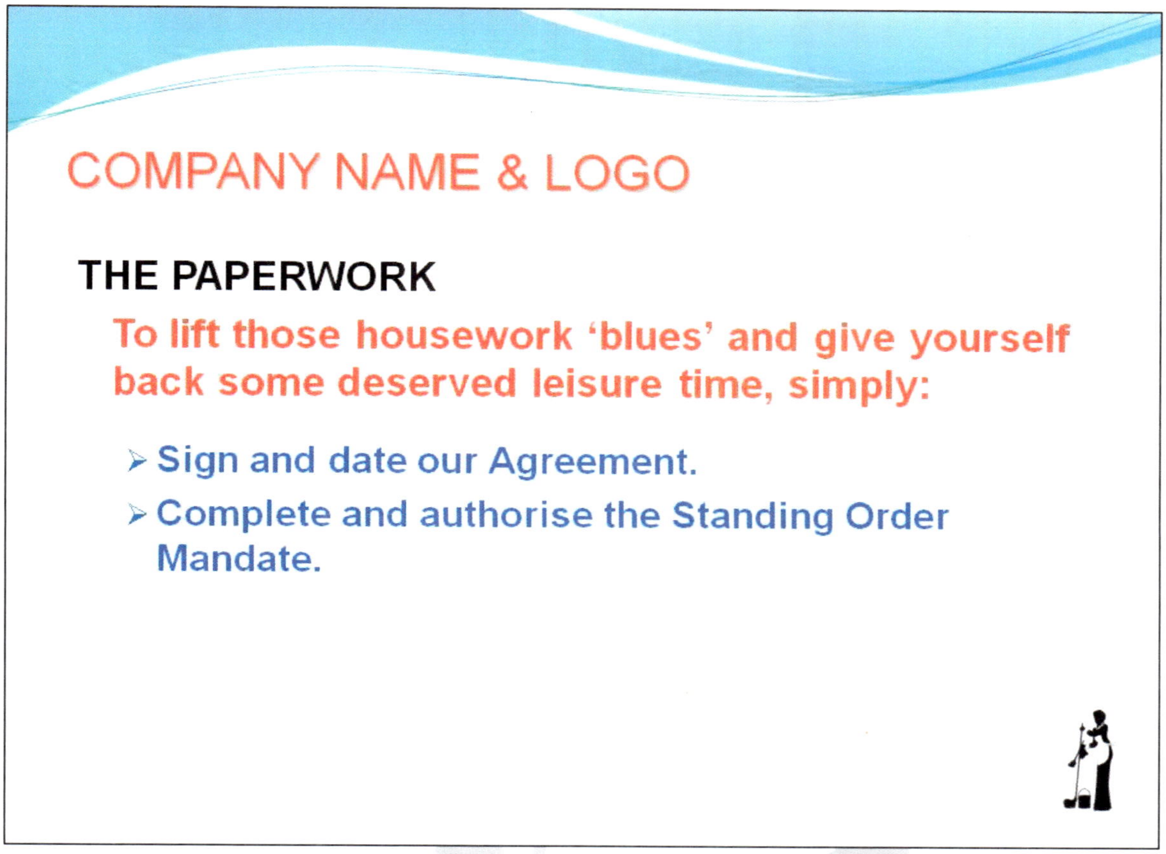

This final slide is your **call to action**.

If you have done a good job in describing your service and dealing with objections you will close 80% of clients at this point and you just need to complete the Client Agreement and Standing Order forms for your client to sign off. However, there will always be some clients who 'want to think about it'. If they say this I normally try to tease out what they need to think about as it can often be an objection that they haven't voiced yet.

When you do this, do it in a helpful rather than in a confrontational style. You could say something like 'is there anything you would like me to explain in more detail? If they are still not ready to sign simply ask when they expect to make their decision. I think you are entitled to ask this as you've probably spent the best part of an hour explaining your service to them.

I would then leave them your client booklet and client agreement / standing order mandate for approval. I would say something like 'Thank you for seeing me today Mrs Smith and I understand you need more time to think about our service. Let me just leave you our booklet and paperwork for when you're ready to go ahead'

After leaving the meeting I would make a note in my diary to call her the day after she said she will be making her decision. I would then telephone and say something like 'hello Mrs Smith, it's Mike from (insert company name). This is just a quick courtesy call to see if you've made any decision about recruiting a cleaner?' If she says she wants to go ahead remind her that she just needs to sign and return the client agreement and standing order mandate. If you are in the area you could even offer to call round to collect the paperwork.

If she has decided not to use your services you should try to find out why as it may help you to modify your presentation or learn about your competition if they won the business. I would then end the call by saying 'I appreciate your feedback Mrs Smith, if you feel we can help you at any time in the future please don't hesitate to contact us'. Always leave the door open as you never know when she might change her mind.

Dealing With Objections

As you go through your presentation you must learn to deal with any questions or objections that might arise. Let's look at a few objections you may encounter and how you might respond:

Objection: "A three month contract is too long"

Reply: Oh, I didn't realise that you were only looking for a temporary cleaner? Our service is for longer term clients who want a regular cleaner, as we take a lot of trouble to find you the right cleaner to match your requirements. Also our cleaners are usually looking for assignments lasting months or years, rather than just a few weeks. Because of this I'm sure you realise that 3 months is the minimum period we can work to.

Or

I understand your concern Mrs X. Would you take our service if we offer you a monthly rolling contract? If she says Yes you could change the contract and standing order to reflect this shortened period.

Obviously don't make this offer unless you have practiced changing the client agreement and the standing order form.

Objection: "What if I don't get on with the cleaner I'll be stuck with her"

Reply: Don't worry, if you don't get on with the cleaner we will provide a replacement.

Objection: "But you've only just set up your service, I may be paying even though you haven't provided a cleaner"

Reply: I understand your concern but we don't charge any fees until we've allocated you with a cleaner. Also if your regular cleaner cannot work for any reason we will provide a replacement within 7 days or we refund your fees.

Objection: "Why do I have to continue paying your fees if I have the same cleaner?"

Reply: The fee is paid to retain our services and the cleaner's services. It takes a lot of time and effort to find and recruit acceptable cleaners for our database - in fact 90% are rejected. Also, don't forget that when your cleaner is absent through sickness / holiday or decides to leave your employment, we will find you a suitable replacement.

Also don't forget we provide valuable insurance cover and carefully monitor cleaner's hours on your behalf so you don't have to worry about having to deduct tax and national insurance.

Remember that objections are really buying signals. Deal with them effectively and you will be closer to signing up a new client. As you gain more experience you will become better at dealing with objections.

Top Tip: Practice handling objections by getting a friend or relative to play the part of the client.

Client Agreement

Your Client Agreement is a legally binding document which defines the contract that exists between you and your clients. It spells out the precise services you will provide to them and the fees they will pay you.

Like all contracts it is an important document to get right because it prevents misunderstandings and possible legal disputes. For example, suppose one of your clients tries to strike up a private arrangement with her allocated cleaner, by cutting you out. One way to prevent this is to predefine in the client contract the level of compensation if this happens. In fact good contracts should actually prevent the need for litigation because responsibilities and actions are clearly defined from the outset.

It is highly recommended that you carry out your own contract assessments with a qualified lawyer to come up with your own terms and conditions that suit the particular operations of your business and the current laws of the country you operate in.

FRONT SIDE OF CLIENT AGREEMENT FORM:

Agreement No:

Add Your Company Name
and Details Here

CLIENT AGREEMENT

This agreement is subject to the terms and conditions overleaf
This Agreement only becomes binding when it has been signed by both parties.

Completed by Client

Contact Details

Name: ____________________

Address: ____________________

____

__________ Postcode: __________

Home Tel. No: ____________________

Work Tel. No: ____________________

Mobile Tel. No: ____________________

Alternative Contact(s): ____________________

How did you hear about our us?
Please delete as applicable
Leaflet/Newspaper Advert/Recommended/Other

Your Requirements

Preferred Day(s): ____________________

Hours required per week: ____________________

Number of visits per week: ____________________

Detail any special needs or information:

____

____

____

Do you require ironing (Y/N): ____________________

Type of Premises: ____________________

Will you be giving out keys (Y/N): __________

Any special security/alarms? (Y/N): __________

Any pets? Please specify number and type:

____

Completed by Company Representative

Payment Details

Hours per Week: ____________________

Gross Hourly Rate: ____________________

Payment per Quarter: ____________________

Bill from Date: ____________________

Bank Mandate Posted (date): ____________________

Additional contract terms or special requirements:

____

____

____

____

____

Signatures

I/We agree that this agreement, subject to the terms and conditions overleaf, shall continue for a minimum period of one calendar quarter and continue indefinitely thereafter unless, I/We cancel in writing by giving one months notice in accordance with the terms and conditions overleaf.

Signed by: ____________________
(The Client)

Date: __________

Signed by: ____________________
(The Company)

Date: __________

Now let's look at the form and how it is completed, starting with the Client details on the left hand side. I usually pre-fill as much of this as possible, from the Client Enquiry form, before the meeting with client. It saves time and assumes the client wants to go ahead which sets the right tone for the meeting.

Contact Details.
Self explanatory.

How did you hear about us?
We use this to find out what advertising is working. Also if you are running a client referral incentive scheme you need to reward any referring client.

Your Requirements
You will use this information to find a cleaner that fits the client's profile. For example you may need a cleaner that is willing to do ironing or a cleaner that doesn't mind pets. Now fill in the information on the right hand side:

Hours per Week
The average number of hours that the cleaner is expected to work per week.

Gross Hourly Rate
This is the cleaner's hourly rate plus your services fee. For example £8 (to cleaner) + £2.50 (to your company) = £10.50

Payment per Quarter
This is your quarterly services fee, calculated as number of hours per week x 13.

Bill from date
You need to leave this blank until you know that the cleaner you allocate has met with the client, because under the terms of the client agreement this is when the first quarterly fees are payable (i.e. on allocation of the cleaner). Reassure the client that you will not forward the standing order to the bank until they meet with their allocated cleaner. As soon as the client and cleaner have met simply add the meeting date to this field and the standing order form. Then you can send the standing order form to the bank and receive your first fees.

Bank mandate posted
This is the date you send the standing order form to the bank.

Additional contract terms
Add any special requirements not covered elsewhere in the agreement. You can also use this section to add additional contract terms, should this rare eventuality occur. For example the client may say that she only needs a cleaner for 9 months of the year because she has a holiday home.

Length of Agreement and Signatures
The length of the agreement is a minimum of 90 days. If your client decides it's not for her after 2 weeks she is not entitled to any rebate unless of course you have failed to provide her with a cleaner in that period. After the initial 90 days the contract continues indefinitely unless the client provides you with 1 month's notice. Of course you are free to set your own terms if you are uncomfortable with this.

Finally get the client to sign and date the agreement before signing and dating it yourself.

Terms of Business

What are they?

Your Terms of Business (sometimes known as Terms and Conditions) explain how the contract with your client operates. I recommend you print them on the reverse of your Client Agreement.

Why are they important?

Having Terms of Business is important because if you get involved in a dispute or any litigation with your clients, they will provide the basis upon which the contract is interpreted. You need to understand your client agreement and each of the terms and conditions in case your client asks you to explain something.

Please be aware of the evolving nature of case law and regulations, so drawing up your specific Terms of Business and keeping them up to date is very much the province of a qualified solicitor.

Top Tip: Your competitors' terms and conditions are sometimes available for download from their websites. However, don't be tempted to copy them word for word as they are unlikely to exactly match how you run your business and also you could be sued for copyright infringement.

Disclaimer:

I am not a qualified lawyer therefore the general guidance I provide below should not be construed as professional advice. It is your responsibility to ensure your Terms of Business are fit for purpose and meet the specific requirements of how you will be operating your business. Always consult a qualified lawyer if you are unsure how to construct your Terms of Business.

Here is my general guidance:

Terms of Business usually start by defining the parties involved and expressions used in the contract. For example it might look something like this:

DEFINITIONS

The meaning of terms used in these Terms of Business are shown below:
'The Company' – (Insert Your Company Name)
'Client' – the person(s) named on the front of this Agreement for whom The Company has agreed to provide the Service(s) in accordance with these Terms of Business.
'Services' – the referral Services to be provided by The Company to the Client as specified in this agreement.
'Cleaner' – the individual(s) introduced to the Client by The Company
'Fee' – the agreed amount payable by the Client to The Company for the Services provided.
'Allocate or Allocation' – the date when the first Cleaner allocated by The Company meets with the Client for the first time.

These are the sole Terms of Business of The Company and shall govern all transactions between The Company and the Client unless otherwise expressly agreed in writing by The Company. A space is specifically provided on the front of the Agreement for this purpose.

You would then typically move onto how the service will be provided. This is where you explain the services provided by your company. Here a list of points I'd recommend you consider:

PROVISION OF THE SERVICE

In return for a quarterly retainer you provide your clients with access to your database of vetted and approved domestic cleaners. Please note that the timeframe may need changing, for example if you choose to be paid monthly rather than quarterly.

Explain that each Cleaner provided is thoroughly vetted and if requested by the Client you are happy to disclose the vetting procedure used in individual cases.

I'd recommend you reserve the right to make variations in the supply of your service as you consider necessary in the interests of improving the Services

Next you need to cover the important subject of payment. Here a list of points I'd recommend you consider:

PAYMENT

Frequency of payment. You are paid quarterly in advance by standing order mandate as detailed on the front of the Client Agreement form. Please set your own time frame based on how often you want to be paid, for example you may opt for monthly payments instead.

If the agreement is terminated by the Client no rebates will be given for fees paid in advance.

Spell out how long the contract lasts for - usually an initial period of 3 months and after that the client can give 1 month's notice in writing to terminate the agreement.

The Client is responsible for paying any Cleaner in cash (or by any other method agreed in writing by the Client and the Cleaner) weekly in arrears at the agreed hourly rate.

Explain how it is the Client and Cleaner's responsibility to complete a Cleaner Earnings Receipt Record to maintain a record of the Cleaner's pay and hours worked. This form must be kept for 6 years for tax purposes. Also explain that the Client must provide a copy of the Cleaner Earnings Receipt Record when you request it or when claiming a rebate.

If the Client cancels the Cleaner with less than 24 hours notice or no notice at all, they should pay the Cleaner a compensation payment (£5 recommended).

If the Client is to allow the Cleaner the keys to their property, then the Client is responsible for obtaining from the Cleaner a Key Security Deposit for the amount specified on the Key Security Deposit Form.

Next move onto your obligations under the contract; in other words the service you will be providing in return for the client paying you an agency fee. Here a list of points you should consider including:

OBLIGATIONS OF THE COMPANY

After the approved client contract and standing order mandate have been returned, you will do your best to find a suitable Cleaner from your database of vetted Cleaners and allocate them to your Client.

Prior to taking on any Cleaner, the Client will be able to interview the Cleaner and confirm acceptance or ask for another candidate.

After the first candidate has been interviewed the client's standing order mandate can be sent to the bank for processing - this is the point in the contract when allocation is said to have taken place i.e. this is when you may send the standing order mandate to the Client's bank.

The Company will use its reasonable endeavours to reply promptly to any queries of the Client and assist in arranging interviews between the Client and a prospective new or replacement Cleaner(s).

Should the Client decide to cancel the Agreement before a Cleaner has been allocated to the Client, a £20 cancellation fee is payable except where such cancellation is due to The Company's failure to allocate a Cleaner.

If requested you will provide the Client with references for clients they have interviewed.

Just as your agency has obligations, so too does the client have obligations to fulfil under the contract.

Here's a list of points I'd recommend you consider including:

OBLIGATIONS OF THE CLIENT

The Client becomes the employer of the cleaner after she takes the cleaner on.

Giving clear and direct instructions to the Cleaner as to cleaning times, hours to be worked and duties to be performed.

Making correct and timely payments direct to the Cleaner at the agreed hourly rate.

Ensuring the duties of the Cleaner are strictly limited to the interior cleaning / ironing.

Terminating the employment of the Cleaner.

The Client must keep you fully informed by giving at least 48 hours notice of any changes in requirements relating to:

- the days or hours worked by a Cleaner
- any complaint about a Cleaner which results in the Client wishing to appoint a new Cleaner
- any Cleaner absences to enable The Company to take appropriate remedial action.

The Client must give at least 24 hours notice to the Cleaner of any changes to working times or material changes in duties.

The Client must supply all the necessary cleaning / ironing equipment and cleaning materials including a working vacuum cleaner and a fully operational steam iron and ironing board (if ironing is required).

The Client must also provide appropriate Health and Safety equipment including access to a first aid kit.

To prevent any misunderstanding about who is responsible damage and the extent of insurance claims you should include an Insurance clause. Here are some example clauses I'd recommend you consider. Obviously amend, add or omit these depending on the cover provided by your particular policy.

INSURANCE

As a courtesy to the Client each Cleaner introduced by the Company and employed by the Client will be covered by an insurance policy which includes public liability cover providing for a maximum payment of £ (insert your level of cover) This covers damage to or write off of the Client's property provided that this damage or loss is caused by the negligence or omission of the Cleaner.

The Company will only cover loss or damage to the property if and to the extent that the loss or damage is of a value in excess of £ (insert your excess level).

The Company will not accept liability for any claims under £ (insert amount) which are hereby excluded. Where any claim is of a value in excess £ (insert amount) the Client shall be liable to pay the first £ (insert amount) of any such claim.

The Client is the employer of the Cleaner and must ensure that their household policy provides Employers liability cover in respect of domestic employees with a recommended level of cover of £10,000,000.

The Company's insurance policy does not cover theft of property or possessions or loss or damage caused by bleach or any substances containing bleach.

The Client acknowledges and agrees that The Company does not have access to police or criminal records when vetting the Cleaners and cannot be liable for false or misleading information provided by Cleaners in relation to such matters.

The Company's insurance policy is subject to a number of further terms and conditions. A copy of The Company's insurance policy will be made available upon request.

The Company's insurance ceases immediately the Client's fees are in arrears.

In the event of a claim the Client must comply with the claims procedure including making a statement relating to the circumstances and value of the damages, supplying receipts / quotes for repair / replacement and liaison with the insurance broker appointed to handle the claim.

Any insurance policy taken out by the Client may void the insurance policy referred to in this clause in which event all damage and loss will only be recoverable under the policy of the Client.

Another important aspect of your contract is to specify any exclusions for liabilities that may arise.

Please be aware that though you may try to limit or exclude your liability, it will be for the regulatory authorities and Courts to decide if a particular clause is fair or not. I recommend you discuss the following areas with your solicitor:

EXCLUSION OF LIABILITY

Loss or damage to the Client or their goods or property caused by your company or by your servants and agents.

Consequential or indirect losses suffered by the Client caused by your company or by your servants and agents.

Consequential or indirect losses suffered by the Client caused by failure of the Cleaner to comply with their contractual obligations or through their negligence.

Failure of, or delay in, performance of any contract due to:

- the imposition, application or enactment of any law or statutory regulation
- strikes and lock-outs
- an Act of God or natural disaster or other cause of occurrence

No liability accepted when the Client is in breach of any obligations to your company.

Failure of any Cleaner to return keys or any consequential loss that may arise as a result.

Inevitably all good things must come to an end at some point in time so you need to spell out how and when you or your client may terminate the agreement. Here a list of points I'd recommend you consider:

<u>TERMINATION</u>

I recommend you should give your clients no less than one month's notice of termination.

Similarly you should make your Client aware that they can terminate the Agreement by giving not less than one month's notice in writing to the Cleaner and The Company.

You need to stop your Clients from terminating your contract and then employing the Cleaner privately. Here's an example clause that you could use:

For a period of 12 months following termination of this Agreement the Client will not employ or use the services of any Cleaner who is or has been contracted as a cleaner through the Company. If the Client is found to be in breach of the above clause it is agreed an immediate compensation fee of £ (insert amount) will be paid by the Client to The Company.

You need to stop your Clients from introducing your Cleaner to their friends and family without going through your company. Here's an example clause that you could use:

The Client will not refer any Cleaner introduced by the Company to any other person , except through the Company. If the Client is found to be in breach of the above clause it is agreed an immediate compensation fee of £ (insert amount) will be paid by the Client to The Company.

Finally terms and conditions are usually ended with some general clauses dealing with interpretation of the contract and the law. Here are some examples you may wish to discuss with your solicitor:

<u>GENERAL</u>

This Agreement is the entire Agreement between the Company and the Client and no variation of this Agreement shall be effective unless such variation is in writing and signed by both parties. This Agreement replaces any relevant existing Agreement between the Client and The Company.

No delay or failure on our part to exercise or enforce any rights or remedies pursuant to the terms of this Agreement shall constitute a waiver of such rights or operate to prejudice the exercise of any such rights at any time thereafter.

If any provision of this Agreement shall be found to be void, invalid or unenforceable the rest of this Agreement shall remain in full force and effect notwithstanding any such invalidity or unenforceability.

Any headings to Clauses or Sub Clauses are for convenience only and shall not affect the interpretation or construction thereof.

These Terms and Conditions shall be construed in accordance with and governed by UK Law and subject to the jurisdiction of the UK Courts.

Client Standing Order Mandate

Receiving your fee payment via standing order offers some major benefits:

- You are paid quarterly in advance, which is fantastic for cash flow.
- You greatly reduce credit control problems. Having to invoice clients quarterly and chase for payment would be a real hassle if it wasn't for good old standing order mandates.
- Your clients are less likely to cancel because payments are made automatically, that way they don't have to make a conscious decision to renew every quarter.
- Payment processing is made easy as there is no need to pay cheques into your bank account.
- Bank charges are reduced.

Clients are familiar with standing order mandates so there should be little resistance on their part, especially when you explain that they have full control over payments. Unlike Direct Debits where the payee can vary the amount taken. Occasionally you will get a client that wants to pay you by cheque and you may be tempted to accept this arrangement, but it really is more hassle than it's worth even if the client pays on time. If they won't budge tell them that your service fees are discounted to take into account the reduced administration of standing order payments. Advise them that if you accept payment by cheque your rate would have to be increased by 50 pence per hour. If they are willing to pay this, tell them you will accept payment by cheque but you will require them to provide 3 post dated cheques to cover quarters 2, 3 and 4. Advise them that you will not cash the cheques until they are due but this would be a stipulation because it will avoid you having to send out reminders. If they are still with you after the first year you will have to write to them for 4 more cheques or encourage them to move to standing order payment for a discount (i.e. your normal rate) but at least you would have earned an additional premium for the hassle.

I recommend you use a 2 part NCR form for your standing order mandate as it looks far more professional and saves time as you should always leave a copy with your client. The Standing Order Mandate should be the final bit of paperwork to complete. The client should have no reservations signing this as you have already explained how your service works with fees being taken quarterly in advance. Let's now go through the various fields on the form and how and when they are completed.

The top 5 boxes on the form contain the client's bank details which you can either ask her to complete or, if she is struggling, you can offer to do it for her. You can get this information from the client's cheque book or bank statement. The account name(s), account number and sort code are also available on their debit card.

The next information on the form relates to your company's bank details, and this should be pre-printed on the form to prevent errors. It tells the client's bank where to pay your fees.

The final boxes relate to when and how much money is to be paid each quarter. These fields are completed by you as follows:

In the Sum of £
Add the appropriate quarterly fees. I would recommend you have your Schedule of Charges (see page 18) handy to quickly calculate how much is due, based on the estimated weekly hours required by the client .

Amount in Words
Simply write the amount payable in words.

Payable On
You need to leave this blank until you know that the cleaner you allocate has met with the client, because under the terms of the client agreement this is when the first quarterly fees are payable (i.e. on allocation of the cleaner). Reassure the client that you will not forward the standing order to the bank until they meet with their allocated cleaner. As soon as the client and cleaner have met simply add the meeting date to the standing order form. Then you can send it to the bank and receive your first fees.

And thereafter until cancelled by me in writing
Simply repeat the amount payable each quarter. It's the same as the 'in the sum of box'.

On the
You need to leave this blank until you know that the cleaner you allocate has met with the client. The 2 digits should be identical to the first 2 digits of the 'Payable on' date. For example if the client and cleaner meet on 10/12/12, you would use 10th.

Signature 1 & Signature 2
When your client signs here it means they authorise their bank to pay you the agreed amounts on the dates and intervals specified. If your client has a joint bank account it may require both account holders to sign, otherwise get her to sign box 1 only.

Date
The date of signing.

Reference
You should add a unique reference here which the bank will use when they pay you. This is essential or you will have great difficulty in recognising which clients have paid you. I would recommend you use the client agreement number.

A Specimen Standing Order Mandate is shown below:

Quarterly Standing Order Mandate

Add your company logo here

Please complete in BLOCK CAPITALS

To: Bank plc (name of your bank)

Branch Address: ______________________________
______________________________ Postcode: ______________

Account Name: (As shown on your cheque)

Account Number:

Sort Code: - - (6 digits) (Top right corner of cheque)

Please make payments to:
Bank: (Add your details here)
Sort Code: (Add your details here)
Account Name: (Add your details here)
Account No: (Add your details here)

In the sum of: £

Amount in words:

Payable on: / / (Date)

And thereafter: £ on the day of every third month (quarter) until cancelled by me in writing.

Signature1 Date:

Signature 2 Date:

Important Note To Standing Order Clerk at the paying bank:
Please ensure the full reference below is quoted on all payments.

Reference:

Note to Client
You may wish to retain a copy of this mandate for your own records, but be sure to return the original to (Insert your company name) and NOT TO YOUR BANK, as we first have to enter in the reference shown above.

Add your company contact details here.

Client Information Booklet

This useful booklet provides clients with valuable information including:

- How your service operates.
- Advice on how to get the best out the cleaners you allocate.
- The client's obligations as the cleaner's employer.

A copy of my Client Information Booklet (without the notes) is shown as Appendix C. You are free to use the booklet, but make sure to amend it where necessary to suit your own business.

Now let's look at the booklet content in detail:

What the booklet says:

INTRODUCTION & WELCOME

Welcome and thank you for considering us to fulfil your domestic / cleaning and / or ironing needs.

This information booklet compliments the Agreement you have signed or are about to sign. It is designed to tell you how we operate and to help you get the best out of our service and the cleaners we introduce to you. We recommend you take time to read this booklet as it contains lots of valuable information and tips to ensure everything goes smoothly from day one.

Why we say it:

Self explanatory really - we want portray ourselves as professional organisation.

What the booklet says:

OUR ROLE

(Add a small preamble about you and your business).

In simple terms our main function is to provide our clients with cleaners wanting to work in the domestic sector. It sounds simple, but in reality we have to put in a significant amount of effort to find suitable cleaners who are able to pass our thorough vetting procedures. In fact we expect 90% of cleaners applying to join our database to be eliminated as unsuitable for one reason or another. We value our reputation and will not compromise on quality.

Why we say it:

We want clients to know we do a thorough job and that finding good and vetted cleaners is not easy. We want them to feel we earn our fee.

What the booklet says:

GETTING STARTED - THE PAPERWORK

To enrol with us we need you to complete, authorise and return our Client Agreement and Bank Mandate forms, which came with this Client Information Booklet. You should send us the top copy and retain the bottom copy of the forms for your records. Upon receipt we will immediately commence the process of matching your particular requirements to cleaners on our database. If we find a suitable match we will ask them to contact you to set up an initial meeting (see Allocation of Workers to Clients). If we cannot find a suitable match we will specifically recruit for your particular needs, though obviously this may take a little longer.

Why we say it:
Sometimes clients do not sign up on the first meeting so we want them to know how to proceed when they are ready to make a decision.

What the booklet says:
OUR AGREEMENT & FEES

In simple terms our agreement is a 3-month rolling contract with a 1-month written termination notice. We believe this allows a reasonable amount of time for you to try our service whilst providing the flexibility to terminate arrangements if your personal circumstances change or things don't work out. Our fee is based on the average number of weekly hours that you contract with the cleaners we introduce. The more hours that you take the cheaper it gets per hour. It can be likened to membership of a Gym, where you pay for the services even if you choose not to use them. However, we are willing to provide a part fee refund when you notify us that you require a temporary or permanent replacement cleaner but we are unable to allocate a worker within 7 days of your request. To claim a refund, just send us a copy of the completed Cleaner Earnings Receipt Record, showing the period of absence. Our fees are paid in advance through a Standing Order Mandate, however, the form will not be sent to your bank for processing until we have allocated a cleaner to you. Once you have started a cleaner you pay them yourself, either after they have finished each cleaning session in your home, or no later than one week in arrears (see Cleaner Pay & Conditions).

Why we say it:
We need the client to understand how the fee works and that we will endeavour to provide cover for their cleaner. When we are unable to provide a replacement within 7 days they are entitled to a refund of fees for the unallocated period of time. NB/ The client must submit a copy of the completed Cleaner Earnings Receipt Record to claim a refund. This is done for two reasons:

- **It allows us to verify the cleaner's hours against the weekly return she has been making.**
- **Clients are less likely to claim refunds if they have to copy a form and send it off in the post!**

What the booklet says:
OUR PRIME SERVICES & BENEFITS

1) We maintain a database of thoroughly vetted, approved cleaners in order to:

   a. Provide you with a regular worker matching your needs.

      Benefits:
      We take the hassle out of finding and checking the credentials of candidates (see 'How Applicants are Vetted '), leaving you to simply focus on the final recruitment decision.

   b. Provide you with a temporary or permanent replacement if your regular cleaner goes on holiday, falls ill or leaves. We hope your cleaner stays as long as you want them to, however, it is the nature of the cleaning industry that cleaners can be transient creatures that move on every 3 to 6 months. We are sure you do not have the time or inclination to find suitable replacements yourself and that is where we earn our fee.

Benefits:
We will do our best to supply you with replacement worker (if required) so that continuity of service is maintained. In the unlikely event that we are unable to offer a suitable replacement within 7 days of you telling us, we will refund a proportion of the fees paid until we have reallocated a cleaner.

2) We provide induction training for our cleaners to re-enforce safe, secure, productive, hygienic and customer focused working practices.

Benefits:
Cleaners are quickly up to speed. Peace of mind and quality results.

3) We provide a system that facilitates the client / cleaner working relationship and ensures that statutory requirements are addressed. For example we provide standard Task Lists, Key Security Deposit Forms, Cleaner Earnings Receipt Records and separate Guidance Booklets for Clients and Cleaners. We also monitor Cleaners' overall earnings from the work we've given them.

Benefits:
Methodical systems of work and proper arrangements for meeting IR requirements and the safe return of keys. Ensures the relationship with your cleaner is productive and relaxed.

4) We provide ongoing support to handle any difficulties that may arise. For example you may be dissatisfied with your cleaner and require a replacement.

Benefit:
You can rest assured that we are always there to provide advice, assistance and back up.

5) As a courtesy to our clients we provide certain insurances to compliment your own household policies (see full details under Insurances Section).

Benefit:
Should major property damage or accidents occur we provide a safety net.

Why we say it:
We need clients to understand the many benefits of our service so that they are less likely to cancel.

What the booklet says:
HOW AND WHEN TO CONTACT US

Our Hours of Business are 9am to 6pm (Monday to Friday).
Tel. Number: (Add your telephone number here).
We are here to help, so please do not hesitate to contact us if you have a problem.
If we are unable to pick up please leave a message stating your telephone number, preferred call back time and a brief reason for your call. We will contact you as soon as we can. Alternatively if it is more convenient you can e-mail us at (Add your email here).

Here are some occasions when you should contact us::

1. **To confirm acceptance of cleaner.**
Please confirm the agreed start date and if the hours have changed from those stated on the agreement. All relevant information is maintained on our database

2. **To cancel.**
Write to our address giving one month's notice of your intention to cancel the agreement. Also write to your bank to cancel the bank mandate.

3. **To permanently replace your cleaner.**
It sometimes happens that cleaners prove to be unsatisfactory for various reasons. Simply tell us why and we will do our best to find a suitable replacement within 7 days.

4. **To temporarily replace your cleaner.**
Sometimes cleaners will let you down or want to take holiday. Simply tell us what has happened within 48 hours and we will do our best to find a suitable replacement within 7 days.

5. **To increase or reduce hours.**
Please agree this with your cleaner and confirm the new arrangement to us.

6. **To temporarily suspend the service.**
If you wish to temporarily suspend the service (for example: to go on holiday). Simply advise your cleaner, giving them as much notice as possible and confirm arrangements with us.

To report accidents.
If your cleaner has an accident whilst working in your home, which causes damage to your property or injury to the cleaner or others. Please provide relevant details and we will advise you how to proceed (also see Insurances Section for further information).

Polite Request:
It is inevitable that you may feel annoyed if your cleaner lets you down. If this happens please do not get upset with the our staff. Please keep in mind that it is not us to blame but the worker. Simply acquaint us with the circumstances within 48 hours and we will thoroughly investigate matters by contacting the worker. We will either arrange for them to resume their duties or organise a replacement according to your wishes. We will not hesitate to take appropriate action against workers who regularly let down clients. Please remember that it is not easy to find totally reliable cleaners for the rates we recommend.

Why we say it:
We need to manage client expectations. Cleaners can be unreliable - it's just a fact of life.

What the booklet says:

1. We initially carry out a structured telephone interview to assess basic suitability. This eliminates many applicants because they are either unsuitable or are unable to meet the following requirements:
   a. Proof of identification (for example passport).
   b. Proof of address (for example a recent electricity bill, in their name).
   c. Two passport size photographs.
   d. Work permit, if applicable (to demonstrate the right to work in the UK).
   e. Either two written references from previous employers or, in certain situations, we may allow character references from select occupations (for example clergy or teacher).
   We ensure that all references are verified.
   f. Contactable by telephone.

2. Once the applicant has put together the above requirements, we visit them in their own home to carry out a detailed interview and verify the documentation. We choose to visit applicants in their own home as it provides proof of address in conjunction with the documentary evidence. It also gives us an opportunity to review the standard of housekeeping in the applicant's own home! As part of this process we ask applicants to declare if they have ever been convicted of any criminal offences. We also ask them if they would have any objection to us running a Disclosure and Barring (DBS) check on them. A Disclosure is a document containing impartial and confidential criminal history information held by the police and government departments which can be used by employers to make safer recruitment decisions. Obviously if they are reluctant to allow this we would have to take it into consideration! If full criminal record vetting is essential to you we may be able to arrange this on your behalf, with the cleaners permission. However, the process can be slow and you would need to pay fees (currently £25). This tends to be impractical because often by the time the results are received back the Cleaner has found employment elsewhere. You should also be aware that basic disclosure information does not include any spent convictions.

3. We then contact the referees and request specific feedback on the applicant, with particular emphasis on their honesty, reliability and work performance. We keep copies of all worker references, copies of which are available upon request.

4. After successfully completing our exhaustive checks we then ask one final subjective question: Would we be happy to offer this person work in our own home?

ONLY IF APPLICANTS PASS ALL OUR VETTING CRITERIA DO WE CONSIDER ALLOCATING THEM TO CLIENTS. WE ARE CONFIDENT OUR VETTING PROCEDURES PROVIDE A ROBUST METHOD OF FINDING HONEST, RELIABLE AND COMPETENT WORKERS.

Why we say it:

We need clients to feel the workers we recommend are trustworthy and effective. Explaining our process helps to convince them that we earn our fee.

What the booklet says:

ALLOCATION OF WORKERS TO CLIENTS

After we have received the approved client agreement and bank mandate from you we will review our database and match a suitable worker to your particular requirements. We then ask the cleaner to contact you directly to set up a mutually convenient time to meet one another. This is your opportunity to outline the work you want the cleaner to undertake and to see if you get on with them and vice versa. If you are happy with the cleaner you simply need to advise us of the agreed start date and confirm the number of weekly hours required. If you are not satisfied with the applicant, please let us know as soon as possible so that we may find a replacement candidate for your consideration

Why we say it:

It clarifies our allocation process and how the interview works.

What the booklet says:

HOW TO GET THE BEST OUT OF YOUR CLEANER

Task Lists

On your cleaner's first day we recommend that you familiarise her with your home. In each room advise her not only what tasks are to be completed but also how you want them carried out. We have included a Task List Form for this purpose. It is also very important that you point out to the cleaner any cherished or valuable items that you do **not** wish them to clean. A simple tip for specifying the work you want done in each room is to divide it into three sections and then list the jobs out:

- **Upper Level**
  For example: remove cobwebs, clean door tops, ceiling lights and fitments.

- **Mid Level:**
  For example: clean pictures, lamps, ornaments, switches, cupboard doors, surfaces and window ledges.

- **Low / Floor Level**
  For example: carpets, wooden floors, skirting boards, rugs, under furniture and beds.

Obviously some chores might be undertaken on a weekly basis whereas others might be carried out on a less frequent basis.

Why we say it:

The Task List system provides a good way of defining the cleaners duties.
Please refer to Appendix D.

What the booklet says:

Work Priorities

Please be realistic when setting work tasks; this particularly applies if you have a large house but only employ the cleaner for a small number of weekly hours. You may wish to consider prioritising the Task List so that the most important work gets completed in the time available. After a few weeks your cleaner should settle into a routine, leaving you to decide if you need more or less hours to complete the scheduled work. If you do change the hours please remember to advise us.

Why we say it:

Clients need to be realistic about how much can be accomplished in the timeframe chosen. A Sample Task List is included as Appendix D.

What the booklet says:

Best Practice Cleaning Regime

Unless you provide alternative instructions we have advised your cleaner to use the following 'best practice' method of working:

1) Work from the highest level down. In this way any dust / dirt will fall to the floor where it can be vacuumed.

2) For reasons of hygiene we encourage clients to follow a colour coding system to prevent cross contamination. To employ this system you will need to provide the cleaner with appropriately coloured gloves and cloths. We recommend:

- Yellow for kitchen and food preparation areas.
- Pink for toilets, bidets and other sanitary appliances.
- Blue for other low risk areas.

Should you not wish to follow the colour coding system then please consider the supply of a dedicated bathroom / toilet cleaning kit to eliminate cross contamination from high-risk areas.

3) Always work from the cleanest to the dirtiest areas in the house, for example start with the kitchen and work your way through to finish with bathroom(s) and toilet(s).

Why we say it:
We are educating the client in good cleaning practices and reminding them that they need to provide the appropriate tools for the job.

What the booklet says:
Cleaning Equipment and Products

It is your responsibility to provide appropriate cleaning equipment, products and tools for the tasks set, including a fully working vacuum cleaner and steam iron. Nowadays cleaners are not expected to follow outdated cleaning methods such as scrubbing floors on their hands and knees, please ensure your cleaner is provided with correct and modern 'tools for the job' as this will foster a productive and happy worker.

Great care should be taken to prevent the inappropriate use of abrasive cloths and powders, which can scratch work surfaces, sanitary ware, furniture and glassware. We would recommend the use of non-abrasive cleaning products to eliminate this potential problem. Please note that our insurance policy does not cover damage to property where the client has contributed to the damage by supplying inappropriate cleaning materials.

All cleaning equipment and products are different, so please take time to explain:

- How each item of equipment works, for example how to change the dust bag in the vacuum cleaner.
- The safe use of equipment and products.
- Where equipment and products are stored.

Why we say it:
We are advising the client to provide the right tools for the job and to educate their cleaner in their proper use.

What the booklet says:
Checking the Cleaner's Work

Please resist the urge to 'hover' around whilst your cleaner is working as this is likely to be off-putting for both of you. Also, although we want you to make your cleaner feel at home, please realise that prolonged chatting will inevitably mean that less work gets done. We recommend that you initially check the standard of work after each cleaning session before moving to less frequent inspections once you feel more confident in the cleaner's ability. It may take two or three visits for your cleaner to 'tune in' to your exact requirements and develop the optimum cleaning routines for your home. Please be patient, make a note of any deficiencies so that you can diplomatically 'coach' the cleaner before she begins the next cleaning session. We receive few complaints about the competence of workers; however, if persistent problems occur please let us know. Very often competence is a matter of personal preference.

Why we say it:
Again we are providing the client with common sense tips about how to handle the cleaner and we are managing the client's expectations.

What the booklet says:
Door Keys and Home Security System

If you are usually out when your cleaner calls, you will probably want her to hold a door key to she can let herself in. To protect the interests of clients and workers we recommend that you complete a Key Security Deposit Form (provided with this information pack) which confirms the arrangement for the transfer of keys. To ensure there is an incentive for your worker to hand back keys when they stop working for you, we recommend that you take a small deposit (say £10), which is immediately refundable in cash when the keys are returned. The deposit may be paid to you in cash or more usually deducted from the first week's earnings.

If your home is fitted with a security system and it may be switched on when your cleaner calls, you will also need to advise her how to deactivate / reactivate it.

Why we say it:

We introduce the concept of the Key Deposit System which will prevent a lot of unnecessary hassle for you when cleaners leave without giving keys back. A sample Key Security Deposit form is included as Appendix E.

What the booklet says:

Safe Working Environment

As a caring employer you have an obligation to provide a safe working environment. An investment of a little time and a few low cost items will ensure your cleaner operates in a safe environment and the bonus is that you and your family will also benefit from these common sense precautions:

- Maintain a First Aid Kit and show the cleaner where it is kept.
- If you have a fire extinguisher or fire blanket, show your cleaner where it is located.
- If you want your cleaner to work at higher levels, please provide a stepladder or other appropriate equipment. Do not expect them to use chairs or other inappropriate items. We recommend that 2 people are present if working above head height.
- If you expect your cleaner to use potentially hazardous chemicals (for example Oven cleaner) please provide a pair of safety goggles and protective gloves.
- Check that your electrical equipment is in good working order and electrical cables and connections are sound.
- Do not ask your cleaner to work externally (for example cleaning outside windows) as this is not covered by our insurance.

Remember that accidents can happen at any time and prevention is always better than cure.

Why we say it:

We are protecting clients against future claims and cleaners against the risk of injury.

What the booklet says:

Cancellation Gratuity

We recommend that you pay a cancellation gratuity whenever you give workers less than 24 hours notice that you wish to cancel a planned work session or the cleaner is unable to gain access to your home through no fault of their own. For example, you may have inadvertently double locked a door. In this type of situation a minimum payment of £5 should be paid to the cleaner for their travel expenses / wasted time. Please remember that wasted visits cost a lot of money relative to most cleaner's personal budget so it is only fair and proper that they should be compensated.

Why we say it:

We need clients to be aware that cleaners rely on their regular income. It is only fair that a cancellation gratuity should be paid if insufficient cancellation notice is given by a client.

What the booklet says:

Pets

If you have pets please agree how these should be dealt with when the cleaner calls. A pussycat may not present a particular problem unless the cleaner suffers from a cat hair allergy, however, a pet snake may need careful consideration!

Why we say it:

Some clients really love their pets but it doesn't mean their pets are going to love the cleaner or the cleaner is going to love the client's pets.

What the booklet says:

First Day Checklist

This is a useful list of topics to cover on your cleaner's first day:

- Visit each room and talk your cleaner through what you want done and how you would like them to do it. We have provided Task List forms to help with this.
- Identify any cherished / valuable Items that you do not want cleaned.
- Show the cleaner where cleaning equipment is stored and how it works, for example how to empty the vacuum.
- Show the cleaner the cleaning products you are providing and advise if you want them to follow a colour coding cleaning system to prevent cross contamination (see Best Practice Cleaning Regime).
- Confirm arrangements for handover of pay and completion of the Cleaner Earning Receipt Record. We recommend that earnings be handed over at the end of each work session or no later than one week in arrears.
- Complete a Key Security form if you expect the cleaner to let herself in.
- Explain how to activate / deactivate the house security system, if appropriate. Show the cleaner where the First Aid Kit is kept.
- Exchange contact information with the cleaner. You will both need to contact one another at some point in time. We have provided a form for this purpose.
- Agree any special arrangements for pets during cleaning sessions.

Why we say it:

There is a lot of information for clients and cleaners to take in so it makes sense to give them a checklist of things to cover when the cleaner first starts work. This will make things go smoother for both parties which makes for a happy client / cleaner relationship. A similar list exists in the Cleaner Information Booklet.

What the booklet says:

CLEANER EMPLOYMENT STATUS

As stated earlier our prime role is to maintain a database of cleaners, that you have access to as and when required. When we introduce a worker to you they become your employee as soon as they start working for you. This is because you are responsible for

- Setting work tasks and routines and explaining how your equipment works.
- Agreeing the times and days you wish them to work, including the total number of required weekly hours.
- Paying them directly in cash at the agreed rate, at the end of each session, or as decided between you.

An exception to this is if the cleaner has officially declared themselves as Self Employed, which is extremely rare as most workers are part time and do not earn enough money to require such action.

Why we say it:
There needs to be no doubt in the client's mind that they are the employer unless the cleaner is self employed.

What the booklet says:

DEALING WITH THE 'RED TAPE'

The reason you have taken on a cleaner is to make your life easier, therefore, we realise you do not want to be bogged down with red tape relating to PAYE and National Insurance etc. Our answer is to provide the means to avoid the red tape through our worker selection and earnings monitoring system. To understand the system we must first acquaint you with the current income tax and national insurance thresholds:

- Income Tax Annual Personal Allowance 2014-15: £10,000
  This equates to £192 per week
- National Insurance (NI) Lower Earning Limit: £111 per week.

Consequently as long as the worker's cumulative earnings are less than £111 per week, you are not liable for employer's National Insurance (NI) nor are you required to collect employees NI and Income Tax.

We record and carefully monitor workers cumulative earnings from all clients on our database. If you want to find out your worker's cumulative earnings simply contact us. Obviously it is important to advise us if you increase the cleaner's hours or pay them more than our recommended hourly rate, as this will impact on our calculations. In this way we are able to take appropriate action to protect our clients interests. For example, the cleaner may be encouraged to become self-employed if it is projected that they may exceed the thresholds. Please note that It is extremely unlikely that cleaners will exceed NI & PAYE thresholds as in practice they will work less than 11 hours per week.

The above information is our interpretation of current Income Tax and National Insurance information at the time of going to press. For more information we recommend you visit the following website: http://www.inlandrevenue.gov.uk/rates.

Why we say it:
We want clients to tell us about changes to cleaners hours and / or pay. Also it is fair to make clients aware of their responsibilities should the cleaner exceed their income tax and NI thresholds. Obviously it is your responsibility to ensure they do not through careful monitoring and allocation of work.

What the booklet says:

CLEANER EARNINGS RECEIPT RECORD

To maintain an accurate record of cleaner earnings and receipts we have provided you with Cleaner Earnings Receipt Record forms. You simply need to fill in the middle section and ask your cleaner to complete the first and last sections. The form must be used to record each working session. When the form is full you should sign at the bottom and pass the second copy of the form to the cleaner. Please keep the top copy of the form in a safe place, as it is a legal requirement to retain it for six years after the worker has left your employment.

Why we say it:

The Cleaner Earnings Receipt Record is not only a means for the client and cleaner to keep track of cleaners hours and pay, but it also represents an important tax document which the Inland Revenue would use in the unlikely event that they carried out an audit of the cleaner's earning. A sample Cleaner Earnings Receipt Record is included as Appendix E.

What the booklet says:

CLEANER PAY AND CONDITIONS

- **Pay**
  Your cleaner relies on your income, therefore, it is important that you pay her promptly in cash after she has finished each cleaning session in your home, or no later than one week in arrears. Please complete a Cleaner Earnings Receipt Record (see above) to record all earnings and payments.

  Why we say it:

  A client who does not pay on time is being extremely unfair on their cleaner. This will often lead to the cleaner leaving which gives you a problem. If a client persistently pays late you should consider parting company with them rather than potentially losing good cleaners.

- **Holiday Entitlement**
  The holiday year runs from 1st January to 31st December. It is a statutory requirement that employers give their workers holiday pay, currently 20 days per year, plus bank and public holidays (usually 8 per year). For part time workers this is provided on a pro-rate basis.

  For the layman, the precise calculation of holiday pay for part time workers can seem like a complicated business, so we are happy to calculate this for you, if required.

  Why we say it:

  Under the law part-time workers are entitled to holiday pay on pro-rata basis. Often clients and cleaners will come to their own arrangements but if they don't you needs to be able to calculate the appropriate amount of pay due to the cleaner.

- **Holiday Scheduling and Notice**
  We believe the question of when holidays are taken and how much notice either party gives is best left to a local, common sense agreement between clients and cleaners, providing **at least** one week's notice is given. This is particularly important if you want a replacement cleaner whilst your regular cleaner is away.

  Why we say it:

  Self explanatory really. Cleaners cannot expect to suddenly take holiday because the sun is shining; they need to give at least 1 week's notice.

- **Statutory Sick Pay / Maternity / Paternity Pay**
  There is no requirement for you to pay your cleaner sick pay or maternity / paternity pay because you are paying them less than the National Insurance lower earnings limit.

Why we say it:
The client needs to be aware that they are not liable for sick pay or maternity / paternity pay. In fact the client would probably need a replacement cleaner as soon as the cleaner decides to stop working in preparation for the birth.

What the booklet says:
INSURANCES

One of the benefits of our service is that we operate public liability insurance policy providing the following scope and levels of cover:

- **Public Liability: £ (insert amount) per claim.** Covers personnel injury and damage for which we can be held legally liable caused by the negligence or omission of the cleaner.

The cover only operates if our fees have been paid in advance as detailed in the our Agreement.

The purpose of our insurance is to provide cover for major damage or disasters. It is not intended to cover minor accidents and low value breakages. The policy has an excess of £ (insert amount), therefore, we and our insurers cannot accept liability for claims under £ (insert amount), which are excluded. For claims in excess of £ (insert amount), you will be liable to pay the first £ (insert amount) of each claim.

Theft of belongings cannot be and is not covered under our insurances.

For full details of insurance cover and exclusions please refer to our Client Agreement. You are also recommended to check the scope of cover provided by your own household policy.

Like any insurance policy there are terms, conditions and exclusions set out in the policy document, which shall bind you in the event of a claim. We are happy to make a copy of the policy available for your inspection upon request.

Why we say it:
Your clients need to be aware of the extent of your company's insurance cover. When breakages or damage does occur you need to take a view on whether you want to enforce these rules rigorously and risk losing the client or perhaps pay all or part of the excess.

What the booklet says:
REFERRAL REWARDS

We hope you like our service and might recommend us to your friends and relatives. We will pay £20 in Marks & Spencer Vouchers for each introduction you make to us leading to new clients taking our services.

Why we say it:
If you work out the marketing cost of signing up each new client you will probably find it exceeds £20, so this is cheaper alternative. Also this type of referral is going to be a lot easier to convert because your client has already recommended you.

The Client / Cleaner Conundrum

What comes first the chicken or the egg?

When you're just starting out it's difficult to know whether you should recruit cleaners first and then promote your services to get clients or vice versa.

Cleaner found but you need clients.....

Let's say you find a suitable cleaner in your target area but you don't have any clients near-by that she can service. First of all you will need to be honest with the cleaner that you have just started your business and may need a week or so to find clients who are close to where she lives. If she has a car her definition of 'close' may mean within 3 or 4 miles. If public transport is not so good or she can only get there by walking, then within 1 mile may be more realistic. Here are some possible solutions:

- Ask the cleaner if she is willing to drop your client marketing cards through letterboxes in streets that you nominate. Obviously you'll have to pay her for this but if she is looking for immediate cash this may work to your mutual benefit. Let's say she delivers 600 cards, you would expect to get between 2 or 3 responses. Immediately you sign up a client you'll be able to allocate work for your cleaner.

- If the cleaner doesn't fancy delivering the client marketing cards, you'll either have to do this yourself or get someone to do this for you. When I first started out I used members of our family who were happy do it for 'pocket money'.

- Tell the cleaner that you will drive her to clients if they are outside of her immediate catchment area. This will increase the chances of quickly finding work for the cleaner. Don't worry this will only be a short term arrangement until you build up your database of registered cleaners and clients. Down the line you can reallocate cleaners to clients based on the distance from the cleaner's house to the client.

Once you have vetted the cleaner you must try to find her work quickly or she may find it elsewhere.

Client found but you need cleaners .....

Let's say you sign up a client in your target area but you don't yet have any cleaners to service their needs. You must be up front with the client and tell them you are just starting out and may require a couple of weeks to find them a cleaner that meets their needs. To take the pressure off a little bit by assuring them that you will not submit their standing order for payment until you have found someone. Now you have a few options:

- Market for cleaners in the local area by placing ads in newsagent windows.
- Market for cleaners by dropping 'cleaner required' cards through targeted letterboxes.
- Use your first cleaner to service all your initial client requirements even if it means driving her to / from clients houses.
- Do the cleaning work yourself until you have sufficient cleaners to do the work. This is not essential unless you need to earn cash quickly. It is only a stop gap measure whilst you build up your database.

THE DAY TO DAY RUNNING OF YOUR SERVICE

Organisation and Record Keeping

So far I have focussed mainly on the early stages of setting up your service, but now I want to turn my attention to the practical day to day running of the business. You probably realise by now that my style is to be systematic and organised and that's what you need to be if you want to run your business efficiently. Get into the habit of writing down a list of things to do so you can prioritise your work.

Top Tip: Deal with most important and difficult tasks first. When you adopt this approach the routine stuff tends to take care of itself. Always try to put a value on what you are doing - for example losing a client may cost you £400 per year.

Top Tip: If you are running your business as a husband and wife team you should allocate duties according to particular your strengths and weaknesses. Let's face it, some of us are good at 'people' skills whereas others might be better suited to administrative tasks.

Some of the items on your plate will be reactive like finding a replacement for a cleaner that has gone sick and some of it will be proactive like keeping on top of your marketing. Keep a diary to record appointments with clients and cleaners and anything else that has a specific time slot allocated. You may have a fantastic memory but in this business I promise you will forget things if you don't write them down. To underpin this you need to keep detailed records, which will typically be a mixture of computerised and hard copy files. Here are some of the records you'll need to maintain:

Client Enquiries File

You will remember that earlier in the book I advised you to complete a Client Enquiry form when clients ring. This form contains the client's contact information, their worker requirements and the date you are scheduled to meet up with the them, which should also be entered in your diary. I recommend you file your client enquiry forms in a lever arch file by client name alphabetically or by scheduled meeting date (earliest on top). In that way you should be able to locate them quickly.

I would recommend that the day before the meeting you telephone the client to remind them that you are meeting up. Never ask if it's still Okay to meet. Instead I would recommend you say something like 'Hi Mrs Jones, its (insert your first name) from (insert your company's name), I'm just looking at my records and I can't read my own writing, could I just check that you live at 34 Woodland Crescent? After receiving confirmation, just say 'Okay, that's great, I look forward to seeing you tomorrow at (insert the time)'.

Now this approach runs the risk that they may cancel but it does offer certain advantages:

- It will save you some wasted journeys because the client has forgot you are coming.
- It provides an opportunity to re-establish the rapport with the client.
- It makes you look human yet professional.

After your client has signed the Client Agreement and Standing Order Mandate you should move their enquiry form to the Client Files.

Client Files (hardcopy)

I recommend the full documentation for each client be placed on one or more lever arch files or in hanging files within a filing cabinet. Each client's file should include the following records:

- Client enquiry form
- Original signed client agreement
- Copy of signed standing order mandate
- Copies of cleaner earnings receipt records submitted by client, usually when they want to claim a refund.
- Copies of any client correspondence, including refund confirmations.

Whenever you need to find out any information about a client, it is all conveniently contained in one place.

Client Record (either card or preferably computerised)

In addition to the hardcopy client files mentioned above, I recommend you also maintain a one page record of your clients' details and their payment history. This will enable you to call up their summary information quickly and respond to any queries.

For example, let's say a client rings you to say their cleaner is going on holiday for a fortnight and they want a replacement, you can quickly see how many hours per week they require, their preferred cleaning days and whether they need someone who can also do the ironing. From their profile, address and postcode you can quickly match them with a cleaner who lives nearby.

I recommend you use a spreadsheet for this purpose, but you could also use a manual card system. Here is the information I suggest you keep:

CLIENT'S NAME: CLIENT AGREEMENT NO:	
ADDRESS:	
LANDLINE TEL NO.	MOBILE TEL NO.
FEE: £ (PER HOUR)	CLEANER PAY: £ (PER HOUR)
TOTAL WKLY HOURS:	CLEANING DAY(S): / / /
IRONING REQUIRED? YES / NO	SPECIAL REQUIREMENTS? YES / NO (SEE BELOW)
CLEANER 1 NAME:	DATE ALLOCATED:
CLEANER 2 NAME:	DATE ALLOCATED:
CLEANER 3 NAME:	DATE ALLOCATED:
CLEANER 4 NAME:	DATE ALLOCATED:
CLEANER 5 NAME:	DATE ALLOCATED:

PAYMENTS:

JAN 14	FEB 14	MAR 14	APR 14	MAY 14	JUN 14	JUL 14	AUG 14	SEP 14	OCT 14	NOV 14	DEC 14
£	£	£	£	£	£	£	£	£	£	£	£

JAN 15	FEB 15	MAR 15	APR 15	MAY 15	JUN 15	JUL 15	AUG 15	SEP 15	OCT 15	NOV 15	DEC 15
£	£	£	£	£	£	£	£	£	£	£	£

REFUNDS:

JAN 14	FEB 14	MAR 14	APR 14	MAY 14	JUN 14	JUL 14	AUG 14	SEP 14	OCT 14	NOV 14	DEC 14
£	£	£	£	£	£	£	£	£	£	£	£

JAN 15	FEB 15	MAR 15	APR 15	MAY 15	JUN 15	JUL 15	AUG 15	SEP 15	OCT 15	NOV 15	DEC 15
£	£	£	£	£	£	£	£	£	£	£	£

ANY COMMENTS:

Cleaner Enquiries File

Earlier in the book I advised you to complete a Cleaner Telephone Pre-vetting Form when cleaners contact you. This form contains important information like the cleaners contact details as well as how many hours they want to work and locations they are prepared to travel to get that work. At the end of the conversation with the cleaner you give them a list of documentation requirements which they need to put together before they call back. In the meantime you should file these forms away in a lever arch file, alphabetically by the cleaners surname so that when the cleaner calls back you can access their information quickly.

When they call back you should confirm that they have everything you asked them for (this is detailed on the form) and then schedule a meeting with them in their own homes so you can verify they are living at the address given and check the standard of their own housework. After scheduling the meeting you should enter the information in your diary and file the form again for safe keeping.

I would recommend that the day before the meeting you telephone the cleaner to remind them that you are meeting up. Never ask if it's still Okay to meet. Instead I would recommend you say something like 'Hi Ann, its (insert your first name) from (insert your company name), I'm just looking at my records and I can't read my own writing, could I just check that you live at 68 Woodland Drive? After receiving confirmation, just say 'Okay, that's great, I look forward to seeing you tomorrow at (insert the time)'.

Now this approach runs the risk that they may cancel but it does offer certain advantages:

- It will save you some wasted journeys because the cleaner has forgotten that you are coming.
- It provides an opportunity to re-establish the rapport with the cleaner.
- It makes you look human yet professional.

Periodically you should go through your Cleaner Enquiry Forms and discard any potential cleaners who have not contacted you within 6 weeks to confirm they have their paperwork ready. Of course if you have the time and are short of cleaners you could try to contact these people to see if they are still interested, particularly if you have a client in their area that you can entice them with. However, my experience is that if they haven't bothered to get back to you on their own initiative, they are unlikely to be the type of motivated individuals you are looking for.

Awaiting Cleaner References File

After you have visited the cleaner and are satisfied with her documentation and cleanliness you will need to check out her references as described earlier in the book. At this point you will normally compose and print off an original and one copy of the reference request form. The original should be signed and posted to the referees given by the cleaner. A copy of the each reference request form, along with the cleaner's documentation and the cleaner enquiry form should be filed in a lever arch file entitled 'Awaiting Cleaner References'.

If, due to urgency, you are sending a reference request by email instead of post you should print out the email and file it with the other documentation. I would recommend you file cleaner reference request letters by date, as you want to be able to review the file daily and chase up any overdue returns. When references are provided to your satisfaction you should put all the cleaner's documentation in the Vetted Cleaners File (see below).

Vetted Cleaners File (hardcopy)

I recommend the full documentation for each vetted cleaner should be filed on one or more lever arch files or in hanging files within filing cabinets. In essence all the cleaners on this file represent your database of approved and vetted cleaners. Each cleaner's file should include the following records:

- Cleaner telephone pre-vetting form
- Cleaner / ironer application form
- Signed declaration of income form or declaration of self-employment form
- Cleaner interview, vetting and training record
- Original job / character references provided by the cleaner
- Completed reference request letters
- Signed terms of association agreement
- A passport photograph of the cleaner
- Completed cleaner weekly earnings declarations
- Any correspondence between you and the cleaner

Whenever you need source information on cleaners it is all conveniently located in one place.

Cleaner Allocation Record (either hardcopy or computerised)

In addition to the hardcopy cleaner files mentioned above, I recommend you also maintain a one page Cleaner Allocation Record which allows you to quickly keep on top of the process of allocating cleaners to clients, pre and post interview.

I will discuss some practical ways the information on these records may be used later in the book.

I recommend you use a spreadsheet for this purpose, but you could also use a manual card system. The records should be filed alphabetically by cleaners name.

Here is the information I suggest you maintain:

CLEANER ALLOCATION RECORD

NAME:	INTERVIEW DATE:

CLIENT NAME(S)	DATE CLEANER ASKED TO CONTACT CLIENT	AGREED INTERVIEW DATE	INTERVIEW OUTCOME (ACCEPT / REJECT)	AGREED START DATE	AGREED HOURS	CLEANING DAY(S)	CLEANER LEAVING REASON

COMMENTS

Now let's look at the required information and how it is helpful:

Clients Name:
Self explanatory.

Date Cleaner Asked To Contact Client:
Enter the date you contacted the cleaner to ask them to set up the interview with the client. It is important that keep a check that the cleaner does actually contact the client, or you will have an unhappy client on your hands.

Agreed Interview Date:
Enter the date that the cleaner and client have agreed to meet up for an interview. You need to phone the cleaner soon after the scheduled interview to ask the outcome. If they have been accepted you will need to send the client's standing order mandate to the bank so you can be paid. If rejected you will need to find out why and allocate another cleaner to the client for interview.

Interview Outcome:
Either accepted, rejected or thinking about it.

Agreed Start Date:
The date the client and the cleaner have agreed to start the cleaning service from.

Agreed Hours:
This is the number of weekly hours that they agreed at interview. Check this against the original client agreement and standing order to make sure it tallies. If it doesn't, you will need to ask the client to sign a replacement standing order mandate for the recalculated fee.

Cleaning Day(s):
The day(s) that the cleaning will take place. Again make sure it matches the original client agreement and update records accordingly.

Cleaner Leaving Reason
When a cleaner leaves a client it is advisable to record the reason. This is useful for understanding why cleaners leave clients and your business. For example it may highlight that the cleaner's hourly rate is becoming uncompetitive or a particular client is difficult to work with. I would recommend you develop a simple abbreviation system for this or make notes in the comments box.

Cleaner Weekly Earnings Schedule

As explained earlier you must keep an accurate track of cleaners' weekly earnings to ensure their total earnings do not exceed current income tax and NI thresholds. At the close of each week your cleaners should complete and submit a Weekly Cleaner Earnings Record showing the number of hours they have worked for their clients and their total earnings. To help you keep track of this important document I would recommend you keep a Cleaner Weekly Earning Schedule which summarises the information for each cleaner and helps you identify any forms that are overdue. I would recommend that you use a simple spreadsheet for this, as shown below:

Cleaner Weekly Earnings Schedule

Cleaner's Name	Week 1 Earnings £	Week 2 Earnings £	Week 3 Earnings £	Week 4 Earnings £	Week 5 Earnings £	Week 6 Earnings £	Week 7 Earnings £	Etc

(The week numbers simply refer to the 52 weeks in a tax year)

Fee Payment Schedule

It is good business practise to keep a close eye on cash flow, therefore you should maintain a detailed summary of your clients' fee payments. This will enable you to chase clients up if their standing order has not been paid on time. I would recommend you check payments at least once a week by cross referencing your bank statements to the schedule.

All the major banks provide accounts that can be accessed online which makes it much easier to do the reconciliation when you want rather than waiting for a paper statement to arrive through the post.

The actual reconciliation should be a relatively easy process as you know approximately when the standing order is due and you have a record of the payment reference (I would suggest you use the client agreement number which is unique to each client). I would recommend you use a spreadsheet to contain this information but you could also use a manual record if that would suit you better. Here's an example below:

Fee Payment Schedule

CLIENT NAME	AGR. REF	DUE DAY	QTR FEE £	JAN	FEB	MAR	APR	MAY	JUN	JUL	AUG	SEP	OCT	NOV	DEC
Smith	0001	20th	97.50		97.50			97.50			97.50			97.50	
Jones	0002	23rd	130			130			130			130			130
Taylor	0003	27th	65		65			65			65			65	
Bell	0004	30th	97.50	97.50			97.50			97.50			97.50		
Patel	0005	2nd	130	130			130			130			130		
Kerr	0006	3rd	97.50		97.50			97.50			97.50			97.50	

Insurance Policy and Claims File

You should always provide your clients with a copy of your insurance certificate if they ask. This will be a rare event because they have already shown they trust you by allowing you to vet and recommend cleaners. However there will be the occasional client that requires this information so keep the original certificate handy for copying.

This file also contains any claims you make under the policy on behalf of the client.

Day to Day Work Routines

You will find that no two working days in this business are the same. Well variety is the spice of life isn't it? You can pretty much divide your daily activities into two camps:

Proactive Work

These are the regular activities you plan and action without any prompting. They include:

Client Marketing and Advertising:

- Developing your client target areas.
- Designing and printing your client cards.
- Delivering your client cards. You can do this yourself or arrange for this to be done for you but make sure your distribution company is reliable.
- Liaising with newspapers and other advertising media to arrange weekly insertions and negotiate rates.
- Placing advertisements in local newspapers, local magazines and Yellow Pages (annually).
- Making sure your website content is current (for example prices and contact details).
- Setting up and maintaining your free Google Places account. We can do this for you for a nominal fee.
- Setting up and maintaining your free Facebook Business page.
- Setting up other online advertising campaigns if required, including Google Adwords. We can do this for you for a nominal fee.
- Setting up advertisements in speciality directories like www.cleaningdirectory.co.uk
- Keeping under review where your client are coming from so you can channel expenditure to channels that are working and eliminate those that aren't.

Cleaner Recruitment, Training and Admin:

- Designing and printing your cleaner recruitment cards.
- Negotiation and placement of cleaner recruitment cards in newsagent windows and other public areas.
- Liaising with newspapers and other advertising media to arrange insertions and negotiate rates.
- Making sure your website content is current to attract cleaners.
- Interviewing cleaners.
- Vetting cleaners and checking their references.
- Inducting / training cleaners using your worker booklet.
- Making sure that cleaners send you details of the hours worked, per client, per week.
- Keeping under review where your cleaners are coming from so you can channel expenditure to channels that are working and eliminate those that aren't.

Accounts and Credit Control:

- Drawing up and monitoring your annual budget.
- Setting up and maintaining your company accounts system. Your accountant should be able to provide advice on this.
- Checking that clients' standing order payments are being paid on time.
- Issuing client refunds (when you are unable to provide replacement cleaners within 7 days).

Record Keeping:

Keeping on top of filing and record maintenance. A list of recommended records that should be kept is detailed earlier in the book.

Insurance:
Setting up and renewing your company insurance policies. As you expand remember to keep your broker up to date on the number of full time equivalent cleaners you employ.

Reactive Work
These are actions that are generated from unplanned third parties inputs, for example clients and cleaners ringing you. Some of these will be urgent and require immediate attention, whereas others can be recorded and dealt with in a quieter moment. You must learn to prioritise your work according to importance and urgency.

Cleaner Job Enquiries:
This is when you carry out your telephone pre-vetting of the cleaner - you have a Cleaner Enquiry Form for this.

Service Enquiries:
This is when potential clients telephone you for more information about your service or want to set up a meeting - you have a Client Enquiry Form for this.

Typical Cleaner Feedback and Enquiries:
Cleaners may ring for a variety of reasons. Here are some of the most common reasons and the actions you should take:

Documentation Ready:

When the cleaner made her initial job enquiry you asked her to put together various documentation prior to interview.

Go over the list of items you need to see and ask the cleaner to confirm she has everything ready. Then set up a good time to meet with her at her home to verify everything.

Start Date Agreed With Client:

Congratulate the cleaner.

Record the details on the Cleaner Allocation Record.

Complete and post the standing order mandate, which you have been holding on file, to the client's bank.

Client Decreases the Cleaner's Hours:
NB/ this should never be below 2 hours per week or whatever you decide to set as a minimum.

Thank the cleaner for ringing.

Ask if this is just a temporary or permanent arrangement.

Ask if the cleaner is happy with the new arrangement and whether she requires more hours from new clients.

Make a note to call the client to confirm the new arrangements.

If appropriate, send the client a new standing order to approve and return to you.

Bring up the Cleaner Allocation Record and amend the details.

Client Increases the Cleaner's Hours:

Thank the cleaner for ringing.

Ask if this is just a temporary or permanent arrangement.

Bring up the Cleaner Allocation Record and make sure the cleaner is still within the financial thresholds for national insurance and NI. If the cleaner would exceed the limits by taking on the extra hours you must tell the client and cleaner that this is not possible. You should then offer the client an additional or replacement cleaner if required.

If the cleaner's total hours can accommodate the additional hours, call the client to confirm the new arrangements and to advise that you will require them to approve a new standing order mandate unless this is just a temporary arrangement (say 1 to 3 weeks).

Cleaner is Unable to Attend Work:

Thank the cleaner for ringing and find out what the problem is, for example sickness, child care etc.

Find out how long the absence is likely to last.

Bring up the Cleaner Allocation Record to establish which clients will be affected.

Remind the cleaner to advise her clients, if she hasn't already done so.

If the problem is likely to last more than 7 days you will need to contact the affected clients to find out if they want you to find a temporary replacement. If they do you will need to go through your database of cleaners to find and allocate possible matches.

Cleaner Wants To Take Holiday:

Thank the cleaner for ringing and make sure she is giving at least 7 days notice. If she hasn't you need to remind her that she must give 7 days' notice in future so you can find her clients a replacement if required.

Find out how long the holiday is going to last.

Bring up the Cleaner Allocation Record to establish which clients will be affected.

Ask the cleaner if she has told her clients and check if they wanted replacements.

Ring clients to check if they want replacements. If they do you will need to go through your database of cleaners to find and allocate possible matches.

Cleaner Wants To Work More Hours:

Bring up her Cleaner Allocation Record and make sure there is sufficient fat in the system to give her extra hours without putting her over the financial thresholds for national insurance and income tax.

If she is near the limit you will have to explain to her that you cannot offer more work without her registering as self employed.

If she is providing a good service to her clients and you can safely allocate her more work, you should tell her that you will put her top of the list for any new work in her area.

Cleaner Wants To Leave a Particular Client or Terminate Your Agency Association:

Thank the cleaner for calling and ask why and when she wants to leave.

Ask the cleaner if she has already told her client(s).

Remember good, reliable cleaners are not easy to find so you should do you best to see if they can be persuaded to stay. Perhaps it is a pay issue or may be there has been a personality conflict with the existing client which could be dealt with by allocating them to someone else.

If the cleaner cannot be persuaded to stay you will need to find and allocate new cleaners from you database.

Bring up the Cleaner Allocation Record and to find out which clients will be affected.

Contact clients and reassure them that you will find a replacement cleaner as soon as possible.

Cleaner Has Damaged Something In the Client's House:

Thank the cleaner for ringing and confirm that she has told the client.

Find out what has been damaged and the circumstances surrounding the incident.

Contact the client to sympathise and to establish the value of any claim.

Remind the client that your policy is really only there to cover major damage and that an excess applies.

If the client still wishes to pursue a claim you should take a view on whether you wish to cover the loss or refer the matter to your insurance broker.

Cleaner Has Been Approached By Her Client To Work For Her on a Private Basis:

Thank the cleaner for bringing this to your attention and reassure her that you will handle things diplomatically.

Call the client and explain to them that private arrangements which cut your service out are not permissible under the client agreement which she signed.

Remind the client of the benefits of being part of your service.

Remind the client that if she still wants to retain the cleaner but not pay ongoing your fees that they will have to pay a transfer fee of £500 in accordance with your terms and conditions.

Client Not Paying Cleaner On Time:

Thank the cleaner for ringing and reassure her that you will take this up with her client.

Call the client and politely remind them that the cleaner relies on her cleaning income being paid on time. Ask that in future they do not ask the cleaner to wait for payment.

Cleaner Change of Address or Telephone Number:

Thank the cleaner for calling and change their records accordingly.

Ask the cleaner to give her clients the new contact details, if she has not already done so.

Typical Client Feedback and Enquiries:

Clients may ring for a variety of reasons. Here are some of the most common ones:

To Confirm Acceptance of Cleaner:

Thank the client for calling and find out the agreed start date.

If this is the first cleaner that has been allocated to the client you should remind them that you will now forward her standing order mandate to the bank so you can be paid. NB/ In accordance with the client agreement the first payment date should be the interview date not the start date.

Call the cleaner to congratulate her and to confirm the start date.

Remind the cleaner that she must complete and send you details of her weekly earnings using the form provided.

To Increase Hours:

Thank the client for letting you know and ask if this is a temporary or permanent increase in hours.

If it's just a for couple of weeks you will earn 'brownie points' by holding your fee at its existing level.

Bring up the Cleaner Allocation Record and make sure the cleaner would still be within the financial thresholds for national insurance and income tax. If the cleaner would exceed the limits by taking on the extra hours you must tell the client and cleaner that this is not possible. You should then offer the client an additional or replacement cleaner if required.

If the cleaner's weekly earnings allowance can accommodate the additional hours, you will need to advise the client that you require them to approve a new standing order mandate.

If this is a permanent change in hours you should update the Client Record and Fee Payment Schedule to reflect the increased fee.

To Decrease Hours:

Thank the client for letting you know and ask if this is a temporary or permanent decrease in hours.

If it's just for a couple of weeks you can get away with leaving the existing standing order in place and just issuing a cheque refund for the appropriate amount **if the client asks for it.**

If this is a permanent change in hours you should update the Client Record and Fee Payment Schedule to reflect the reduced fee.

To Temporarily Replace Cleaner:

Thank the client for calling and find out why the temporary replacement is required. The cleaner should let you know but they often forget. Assure the client that you will do your best to find a replacement, assuming they have given you sufficient time to do so. Remember your client agreement says that fee refunds are only due if you have not found a replacement cleaner within 7 days.

Bring up the Client Record to check the number of hours required by the client, the specified cleaning day and other details.

Look through your Cleaner Allocation Records to see if you can find another cleaner who may be willing to do the extra hours. Then put her in touch with the client.

If you cannot find a replacement you should let the client know and issue a refund if the period without a cleaner is longer than 7 days.

Clients can often manage without a cleaner for 1 week. In fact they sometimes can't be bothered to 'break in' a new cleaner for just 1 visit.

To Permanently Replace Cleaner:

Thank the client for calling and find out what the problem is. Normally a client will ask for a permanent replacement because their allocated cleaner has given notice. However, sometimes relationships break down so the client will simply ask that you replace the present cleaner with a new one.

If there is a major problem with the cleaner you will need to get to the bottom of it for the sake of other clients that that cleaner may be serving.

If the request occurs in the first couple of weeks of an allocation it may be because the cleaner needs time to tune in to the client's particular requirements. If this is the case you should encourage the client to give the cleaner a little more time to settle in.

If the client is adamant she wants a replacement you will need to advise the cleaner and make sure they tie up any loose ends like handing back the keys, if appropriate.

Bring up the Client Record to check the number of hours required, the specified cleaning day and other details.

Look through your Cleaner Allocation Records to find another cleaner to match the client's requirements. Then arrange for the cleaner to contact the client to set up an interview.

If you cannot find a replacement you should let the client know and issue a refund if the period without a cleaner is longer than 7 days.

Remember to update your Client and Cleaner Allocation Records when a new cleaner is allocated to a client.

To Temporarily Suspend the Service:

Thank the client for calling and ask why they want to suspend the service and for how long. This maybe because they are going on a lengthy holiday, being transferred away on business temporarily or going into hospital for a few weeks. Whatever the reason you should remind the client that your fees should remain in place if they want to use the service again in the foreseeable future. If they ask for a refund you must remind them that your fees are not refundable in this situation. Use the analogy of Gym fees which are paid whether or not you use the service.

To Cancel Your Agreement:

Thank the client for calling and ask why they no longer want to use your services. It may be that they don't rate their current cleaner and are not aware that they simply have to ask for a replacement.

With the best will in the world there will always be some relationships that go wrong or a client's expectations exceed what you can realistically provide.

In these situations it is best to part on good terms for the sake of your reputation. Strictly speaking clients have to give you 1 month's notice or the contract rolls over for another 3 months. That means no refund of fees paid in advance. However, if I think that we have not given the level of service that I would expect to provide I will sometimes take a view on matters and act accordingly.

Remember to keep your cleaner informed and try to find her a new client, assuming you think the cleaner is worth retaining.

Update your Client and Cleaner Allocation Records.

To Report Accidents:

Thank the client for calling and offer sympathy. Remember some items are not valuable but may have deep sentimental value.

Find out what has been damaged and the circumstances surrounding the incident.

Establish the value of any potential claim.

Remind the client that your insurance policy is really only there to cover major damage and that an excess applies.

Encourage them to consider claiming on their household insurance which will often have a lower excess.

If the client still wishes to pursue a claim you should contact your insurance broker who will advise you how to proceed.

If the claim is small (under £100) it will not normally be covered by your policy so you may wish to consider making a full or part contribution towards the claim if it prevents you losing a good client.

You need to talk to the cleaner and ask her to be more careful in future.

Update your insurance file with all the details.

FREQUENTLY ASKED QUESTIONS:

Can I run this business part time?

Yes you can, but it will take you longer to achieve results. When you are out of the 'office' make sure you have a suitable answer-phone message and call clients and cleaners back at the earliest opportunity.

Can I run my business in any postcode area I choose?

Yes you can, you are not limited like a franchise or similar arrangement.

How much initial funding will I require?

How long is a piece of string? You can cut some corners in your initial budget like using your home phone or mobile for a while instead of installing a dedicated business phone. Also you can print your stationery, forms and marketing materials in house on a laser printer rather than having them litho printed. See our Documentation Customisation option by visiting:
http://howtostartacleaningbusiness.org.uk/document-customisation-service/

My personal recommendation would be to use the services of a professional litho printer for your external documents and marketing materials as soon as your budget allows. Inferior quality paper or printing may lose you clients in the long run.

If I order my printing through you how much will it cost?

The most cost effective way to print your stationery and forms would be to consolidate everything into one order rather than raising orders for separate items. Our trade printers offer a 10% discount on already discounted prices if you do this.

I like to think of the business forms and stationery as either being for internal or external use. In general terms those forms that you use in-house can safely be printed on a laser or ink jet printer as they are only seen by you. On the other hand external forms and stationery (i.e. they are seen by clients and cleaners) should really be printed to a professional standard by a proper printing company. This especially applies to legal agreements and other forms where you need to produce duplicates at the time they are completed.

Forms that can be printed internally are shown as **Appendix G**.

Forms and stationery that we recommend be printed externally are shown as **Appendix H**. This appendix also includes price information from our trade printers, so you can prepare an accurate budget. These prices include delivery and minor artwork alterations, like adding your logo and company details, whereas other printers would usually charge you for these extras.

For more information please visit: http://howtostartacleaningbusiness.org.uk/trade-price-printing/

How Long Will It Take Me To Learn and Implement Your System?

My system is designed to fast track you to success. I have distilled all my years of research and practical experience into this book. All the ingredients are there but only you can make it happen. If you are really motivated there is no reason why you couldn't be established and earning your first income within 2 to 3 weeks.

My advice is to take time to read through the book and understand how things fit together. It's not rocket science but like all new learning processes, you may need to break them into bite size chucks so you can digest them before moving on. Soon all the jig saw pieces will come together and you will be ready to rock and roll.

Are there any areas where your system will not work?

This system works at its best when there are sufficient clients and cleaners located in close proximity. For that reason it may not work well in sparsely populated areas or where there is an imbalance of clients to cleaners or vice versa. In other words finding an area which is extremely affluent and rich in clients is no use without a lower paid grouping being in close proximity. Similarly finding an area with an abundance of cleaners is no use unless there are affluent clients nearby who want those services. It's no different to any other business - you must be able to match supply with demand.

Should I register for VAT?

Registering for VAT is not necessary unless your annual turnover is over £81,000 per annum (2014 / 2015). As soon as you expect to exceed this turnover limit you must register with HMRC and start charging VAT on your agency fees. Please note that VAT is not chargeable on your cleaners' earnings.

The disadvantages of charging VAT are that your services fees will immediately increase by 20% (current VAT rate 2014 / 2015) which is unlikely to be welcome with clients. This will also make you less competitive against competitors who do not have to charge VAT.

Alternatively you can absorb the VAT cost yourself, by keep the same services fees. This will mean that your profits will drop significantly (20%) overnight.

The advantages of charging VAT are that your business will be perceived as bigger and you will be able to claim VAT back on business purchases, however overall I would recommend you do not register for VAT until your revenue starts to approach VAT threshold limit and you want to continue expanding your turnover well beyond the VAT threshold.

LEVERAGE THE FUTURE

Let's not run before we can walk, *but dreams can inspire us..........*

Once your business has been established a couple of years and is generating good profits you may wish to consider expanding your business. There are a couple of options open to you:

Take on more administrative staff and expand into new areas. Perhaps you have only been operating in your own town and now want to pick up more business further afield. You just have to follow the same blueprint I have given you but train staff to do it for you.

Alternatively you could follow a franchise route and recruit suitable franchisees to your network. For the privilege of learning how to use your business blueprint your franchisees will pay you an upfront franchise fee and additional ongoing monthly management fees.

You will need to take advice from franchise lawyers and consultants but it can be an excellent way to generate a significant amount of additional revenue. For example, say you sold 200 franchises based on post code territories at £10,000 each, you could generate £2 million.

Okay, some of that revenue would need to be reinvested in training and support of your network, but it would still leave a very sizeable residue. Additionally you could generate ongoing management fees based on a flat monthly rate or as a percentage of revenue. Let's say you take a flat £200 per month from 200 franchisees, it would equate to £40,000 per month!

All this is possible if you are motivated and you develop your brand properly.

For more information on franchising I'd recommend you take a look at the British Franchise Association website(http://www.thebfa.org/Home) where you will find a lot of excellent advice.

LIST OF APPENDICES:

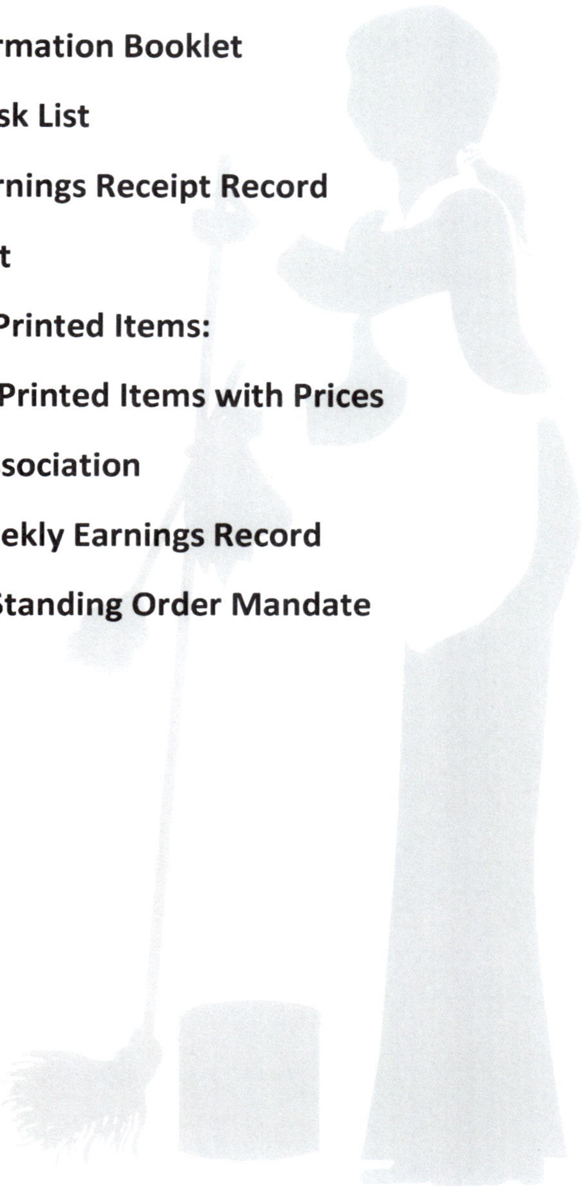

Appendix A - Client Agreement:

Agreement No:

Add Your Company Name
and Details Here

CLIENT AGREEMENT

This agreement is subject to the terms and conditions overleaf
This Agreement only becomes binding when it has been signed by both parties.

Completed by Client

Contact Details

Name: ____________________

Address: ____________________

____

__________ Postcode: __________

Home Tel. No: ____________________

Work Tel. No: ____________________

Mobile Tel. No: ____________________

Alternative Contact(s): ____________________

How did you hear about our us?
Please delete as applicable
Leaflet/Newspaper Advert/Recommended/Other

Your Requirements

Preferred Day(s): ____________________

Hours required per week: ____________________

Number of visits per week: ____________________

Detail any special needs or information:

____

____

____

Do you require ironing (Y/N): ____________________

Type of Premises: ____________________

Will you be giving out keys (Y/N): __________

Any special security/alarms? (Y/N): __________

Any pets? Please specify number and type:

____

Completed by Company Representative

Payment Details

Hours per Week: ____________________

Gross Hourly Rate: ____________________

Payment per Quarter: ____________________

Bill from Date: ____________________

Bank Mandate Posted (date): ____________________

Additional contract terms or special requirements:

____

____

____

____

____

Signatures

I/We agree that this agreement, subject to the terms and conditions overleaf, shall continue for a minimum period of one calendar quarter and continue indefinitely thereafter unless, I/We cancel in writing by giving one months notice in accordance with the terms and conditions overleaf.

Signed by: ____________________
(The Client)

Date: __________

Signed by: ____________________
(The Company)

Date: __________

Appendix B – Worker Information Booklet:

Introduction and Welcome

Thank you for registering with our company and welcome, you should be proud of yourself, as the majority of applicants do not make it this far!

This little booklet is designed to tell you how we operate and to help you make a flying start with the clients we introduce to you. Please read this booklet thoroughly as it contains lots of valuable information and tips to ensure everything goes smoothly from day one.

Contents:

OUR ROLE

Add a small preamble about you and your business

In simple terms our main function is to match people who need cleaners with people who want to work as cleaners. Therefore, we act as a 'middle man' serving both clients and cleaners. It is our clients who pay for our ongoing service through an agreed standing order fee. This ensures that if a cleaner goes on holiday, is sick or decides to leave, we will quickly find them a replacement from our database. The monthly retainer paid to us does not impact on your rate of pay. In fact we realise how important it is to retain workers so we have negotiated with our clients what we believe to be some of the best cleaner rates of pay in the market place today.

WORKER SELECTION

We value our reputation and that is why we take time to carefully vet all workers wanting to register with us. By now you should already be aware that we have asked you to provide a lot of information:

- Proof of Identity
- Proof of Address
- Written References
- Passport Photographs

PLACEMENT WITH CLIENTS

After successfully completing our vetting procedures we will do our best to place you with clients that match your profile in terms of:

- Number of hours you want to work per week.
- Particular days and times you are available to work.
- Places you are prepared to travel to for work.

We will either allocate you to existing clients, whose cleaners have left, or new clients who wish to try our services.

As you prove yourself we will endeavour to find you as much work as you wish.

ARRANGING THE INITIAL CLIENT CHAT

We will provide you with the contact details of the client and ask you to set up a mutually convenient time to visit them for an initial chat. This will give you both a chance to see if it 'feels right' and will also provide an opportunity for the client to explain her particularly requirements. Nine times out of ten a start date will be agreed on this day and you simply need to advise us.

In the unlikely event that this particular client is not for you, please let us know straight away what the problem is and we will arrange to place you elsewhere.

WHEN TO CONTACT US

You may contact us at any time on (add your phone number here). Our normal hours of business are 9am until 6pm, Monday to Friday. If we are unable to answer when your call, please leave a message on our Answer phone, giving your name and contact telephone number, and we will return your call as soon as we can. It is essential to keep us informed in the following circumstances:

- You agree to change your hours with a client.
- You are feeling unwell and cannot attend work.
- You want time off (please give us and the client at least 7 days notice and ask the if they want a replacement whilst you are away).
- You have an accident whilst working in the client's home, which causes damage to their property or injury to yourself or others.
- The client encourages you to leave us and instead work for them directly. This would represent a breach of contract so please let us know in order that we may diplomatically nip it in the bud.
- You want to increase the number of hours that you work.
- The client is not paying you on time.
- You change your address or telephone number.
- Any other situation you feel we should be aware of.

It is in our interests that you are a success and we will do all we can to support you with clients, so please do not hesitate to contact us if you need help or advice.

EMPLOYMENT STATUS AND PAY

You are employed by our clients who are responsible for:

- Setting your work routines.
- Agreeing the times and days they wish you to work, including the total number of required weekly hours.
- Paying you directly in cash at the agreed rate, at the end of each session, or as agreed with you.

You are not employed by us, therefore, we cannot be responsible for your pay. However, whilst you are working for our client(s) you must abide by our Terms of Association.

It is your responsibility to arrange your personal tax affairs. For your information we have included some useful financial information at the end of the guide.

HOLIDAYS

It is extremely important that you let us **and** clients know if you want time off. Please give at least one week's notice and ask the client if they want a replacement whilst you are away. If they do, please let us know straightaway so we have sufficient time to organise everything,

SICKNESS AND UNAVOIDABLE ABSENSE

If you are feeling unwell or need to take time off (for example a family emergency) please notify us and clients as soon as possible. This will enable us to put cover in place, if required by the client. Please note that it is not a requirement for clients to provide sick pay.

CANCELLATION GRATUITY

We recommend to clients that they pay a cancellation gratuity (non obligatory) whenever they give workers less than 24 hours notice that they wish to cancel a planned work session. Whilst this is usually rare, it does sometimes happen that a client forgets to alter arrangements or inadvertently double locks a door. In this type of situation they should pay you £5 for your wasted time).

LEAVING US

Please give us a **minimum of one week's notice**. This will give us a reasonable chance of finding a suitable replacement for our clients. Please don't feel awkward or embarrassed if you want to leave, we promise to accept your decision in a friendly and professional way and besides you may need a reference from us at some time in the future.

KEY SECURITY

One of the first things you will need to do with new clients is to agree how you should access to their property. If the client is usually out during the day, they will probably want to hand over door and security keys (if appropriate). To protect the interests of clients and workers we recommend that you both complete a Key Security Deposit Form (copy available upon request) that confirms the agreement you have made with the client for the transfer of keys. To ensure there is an incentive for workers to hand back keys when they stop working for clients, we recommend that the client take a small deposit (say £10), which is immediately refundable when the keys are returned. This deposit may be paid in cash or more usually deducted from your first week's earnings. For security reasons client keys must be kept in a safe place at all times and you must not write the client's name, address or telephone number on the keys or key ring. When you leave the clients employment you must hand the keys back in person.

CLEANER EARNINGS RECEIPT RECORD

We have provided clients with Cleaner Earnings Receipt Record forms. This is a two-part form to record earnings you have received with that particularly client. This eliminates the need to rely on memories as it records hours you have worked and most importantly the pay you have received or you are owed. You should complete the first and last sections, with the client completing the middle section. This must be done at the end of each working session. When the form is full the client should sign at the bottom and give you the second copy for your records.

GETTING THE BEST FROM YOUR CLIENT:

Task Lists

On your first visit to a client, ask them to walk you through their home describing what they would like done on a room by room. We have provided a Task List (see above) for this purpose. We recommend that clients not only complete the Task List but also talk you through how they want things done. It is also important that you ask the client to point out any cherished or valuable items that they do **not** wish you to clean.

Cleaning Equipment and Products

The client is responsible for providing you with all necessary cleaning equipment and products. All equipment is different so please ask them to show you how their equipment works e.g. how to change vacuum cleaner bags. Also ask them to show you where the cleaning products are stored and how and where you should use them. If you feel the client is not providing the necessary cleaning equipment or products for you to do your job properly, then don't be afraid to diplomatically bring it to their attention. Obviously you will get much more done in the time available if they provide the right tools for the job.

Priorities

On some occasions there may be more tasks on the task list that can be comfortably managed in the allotted time. In these situations ask the client if she wants to prioritise the tasks, so that the more important tasks get undertaken in the time available. Alternatively they may decide they want you to work more hours. Please always inform us if your hours are increased or decreased by the client.

Security Systems
It is important that your client instructs you how to activate / deactivate the security system if they expect you to work in their home whilst they are out.

SAFETY PRECAUTIONS AND GENERAL CONDUCT

It is of the utmost importance that all workers we introduce demonstrate respect for our clients and their property and act in a safe, secure, honest and responsible way at all times. Here is a list of some dos and don'ts:

Respect for Clients
The following activities are STRICTLY PROHIBITED:

a. Smoking, consuming alcohol or eating whilst on client property.
b. Unauthorised use of the client's telephone, equipment or property.
c. Sub contracting your work to friends, relatives or anyone else.
   We need to interview everybody who starts work with a client. Please refer any interested friends or relatives to us so we can interview them accordingly.

Honesty
It goes without saying that the highest levels of honesty are required. This not only applies to clients money and possessions but also ensuring you only claim for the hours actually worked, particularly when the client is not present whilst you are working.

Irons
Always ensure that irons are switched off after use and never place them flat down (even when switched off). If you feel the iron has cooled down enough still take care to position it in an upright position.

Cooker Hobs
Beware of flat-topped cooker hobs. When cleaning, it is easy to brush against a switch or knob and accidentally turn on the hob. Do not rest cloths, magazines or anything else on these hobs. Also take care not to drop anything on ceramic hobs as this may cause them to crack.

Gas
Gas hobs, cookers and fires can all be accidentally switched on or left on by someone unfamiliar with the controls in a strange house. Be extra careful when wiping or dusting the controls and take appropriate action if you smell gas.

Abrasive Cleaners and Smooth Surfaces
Beware of smooth surfaces, for example white sinks and white kitchen surfaces as these can easily mark or chip. Clients do notice these things so please be careful. NEVER use abrasive cleaners or cloths on any surfaces. Check with the client first to see what they use.

Taps
Taps can easily be left dripping and this can lead to serious flooding if the plug is left in the plughole. Be sure to turn off all taps and never leave plugs in the sink.

Security
Unless instructed otherwise by clients ALWAYS LOCK UP SECURELY WHEN YOU LEAVE – be sure to check all windows and doors.

Working at Heights
Do not stand on chairs or other items of furniture to clean high surfaces or to reach something. We recommend that you only undertake such tasks if you are provided with a stepladder or other appropriate equipment. When working above head height always request that the client is present to provide assistance, if required.

Working Outside
Our Insurance does not cover you if you have an accident whilst cleaning the **outside** of a client's house, for example cleaning the outside of windows. Politely decline such work if requested by the client unless the clients household insurance covers you for any accidents and you wish to undertake such work.

First Aid Kit
Ask the client to show you where they keep their First Aid Kit. This is important if you have an accident.

Cleaning Products
Read the manufacturer's safety and instruction labels carefully and only products in the way prescribed. Know what do if you have an accident.

CLEANING ROUTINES

1) Ask the client to list out the work to undertake on the Task List form. To assist the client in compiling their lists you may wish to ask them to consider each room at three levels:

- **Upper Level**
  For example: cobwebs, curtain rails / pelmets, door tops, ceiling lights and fitments.
- **Mid Level:**
  For example: pictures, lamps, ornaments, switches, cupboard doors, surfaces and window ledges.
- **Low / Floor Level**
  For example: carpets, wooden floors, skirting boards, rugs, under furniture and beds.

Work from the highest level down. In this way any dust / dirt will fall to the floor where it can be vacuumed.

2) For reasons of hygiene we encourage clients to use a colour coding system to prevent cross contamination. To enable you to operate this system the client should provide you with colour coded gloves and clothes. We recommend:

- Yellow for kitchen and food preparation areas.
- Red for toilets, bidets and other sanitary appliances.
- Blue for other low risk areas.

If the client does not wish to follow the colour coding system then at least ask them to supply a separate bathroom cleaning kit so that all cleaning products and equipment may be kept in one place thus eliminating the risk of cross contamination.

3) Always work from the cleanest to the dirtiest areas in the house, for example complete the kitchen before moving on to bathroom and toilets.

CLEANING TIPS

Always tidy away before cleaning, for example take dirty dishes to the kitchen and put any loose toys in the toy box.

Always dust before vacuuming, as the dusting process will dislodge any particles onto the floor where they can be hovered up.

A dampened, clean cotton cloth is a very effective duster. To dampen, simply hold the cloth by one corner and lightly mist with clean water from a spray bottle. The cloth should be just damp enough to pick up dust without leaving moisture streaks.

When dusting wall units, first lift and dust any ornaments or other objects, then dust the shelf both underneath and behind. Start from the top of the unit and work your way down to the bottom.

Never dust a warm or hot light bulb with a damp cloth, as you may give yourself an electric shock or shatter the bulb.

An effective way to remove dust from awkward places (for example: louvered doors, telephone keys, carved furniture, etc.) is to use a dampened and clean, soft paintbrush.

To remove pet fur from upholstery use a damp cloth or rubber glove.

On tiled or vinyl floors, sweep or vacuum first to collect crumbs, loose hair and dirt before damp mopping. Start mopping in the farthest corner of the room and work your way toward the door.

To clean the narrow space between kitchen appliances, try using a cloth on the end of a mop or broom handle.

To loosen any baked on food in microwave cookers, place a cup of water inside and set the controls on high for a few minutes. The steam should soften up the splatters for easier removal.

Cooker burner rings and drip pans will be easier to clean if they are first soaked in a sink full of hot, soapy water to loosen the baked spills.

To maintain vacuum cleaners at maximum suction change the vacuum bag as recommended by the manufacturer. Please note that some vacuums eg. Dyson do not have bags but must be emptied when the dirt reaches the level marked on the collection chamber

Poor vacuum suction may indicate a blocked hose, which can easily be checked by disconnecting the hose at both ends and then seeing if a coin will drop through it. If the coin does not fall out there is probably a blockage, otherwise the problem lies elsewhere.

To straighten the fringe on rugs, sweep away from the centre of the rug using a plastic hairbrush.

When cleaning pictures frames, start at the top of the frame, then clean down the sides and across the bottom.

Chrome can be made to gleam by simply using a dry cloth.

Dust may be removed from the front of stereo speakers with the vacuum hose and flat attachment. Be careful to avoid damaging the delicate speaker mechanisms.

Use a power head to vacuum carpeted areas, but never use a beater bar on hard surfaces as it can cause damage.

Cleaning products may be limited to a quality window/glass cleaner,

all-purpose cleaner, tile/grout cleaner and a toilet bowl cleaner.

Never mix two cleaning products together as it may cause a dangerous reaction, for example it may create dangerous fumes.

To avoid damage never put wet cloths, bottles, buckets or damp mops on furniture, carpets, hardwood floors, etc.

Check underneath furniture before hovering to prevent small items such as toys, money, jewellery, etc. being sucked up.

A good way to remove cobwebs is to tie a lightly dampened cloth round the end of a mop or broom.

To clean mini blinds close the slats and dust, then close the slats in the opposite way to dust the other side

Do not spray glass cleaner directly onto picture glass, computer monitors or TV screens. Instead spray a little glass cleaner on a cloth, as this will prevent streaks and keep the spray off areas that might be harmed by direct contact with the cleaner.

Beware when cleaning electrical equipment - always check the manufacturer's manual for instructions.

CLIENT CHECKLIST

This is a useful list of things to cover when you meet the client for the first time.

- Get the client to talk you through what they want done and how they would like you to do it. We have provided your clients with Task list forms to help with this.
- Identify any cherished / valuable Items that the client does not want you to clean.
- Find out where cleaning equipment is stored and how it works, for example how to empty the vacuum cleaner.
- Find out what cleaning products the client is supplying and if they want you to follow the colour coding cleaning system explained in this booklet.
- Ask the client to complete the Cleaner Earning Receipt Record, to cover each session worked.
- Remind the client that you are paid in cash at the end of each cleaning session.
- Complete a Key Security Form if they expect you to let yourself in.
- Find out how to activate / deactivate the house security system, if one is fitted and they expect you to let yourself in.
- Find out the whereabouts of the First Aid Kit.
- Exchange telephone number information with the client. You will both need to contact one another at some point in time.
- Find out if the client has any pets and, if appropriate, agree how these will be dealt with when you call.

INCENTIVE SCHEME

We operate an incentive scheme that pays a fee of £10 for each Cleaner or Client you introduce to us. Some terms and conditions apply so please ask us for further details.

USEFUL FINANCIAL INFORMATION

For financial information we recommend you visit the following website:
http://www.hmrc.gov.uk/individuals/index.shtml

RECORD OF CLIENT CONTACT DETAILS

This form is to record client contact details and work schedules. This is useful if you need to contact clients. For example, if you need to advise them that you cannot attend work.

Name: ____________________ Tel Eve: ____________________
Address: ____________________ Tel Day: ____________________
____________________ Business No: ____________________
____________________ Days: ____________________
__________ Postcode: __________ Times: ____________________
Other Notes: ____
____
____

Name: ____________________ Tel Eve: ____________________
Address: ____________________ Tel Day: ____________________
____________________ Business No: ____________________
____________________ Days: ____________________
__________ Postcode: __________ Times: ____________________
Other Notes: ____
____
____

Name: ____________________ Tel Eve: ____________________
Address: ____________________ Tel Day: ____________________
____________________ Business No: ____________________
____________________ Days: ____________________
__________ Postcode: __________ Times: ____________________
Other Notes: ____
____
____

12

Appendix C – Client Information Booklet:

CONTENTS

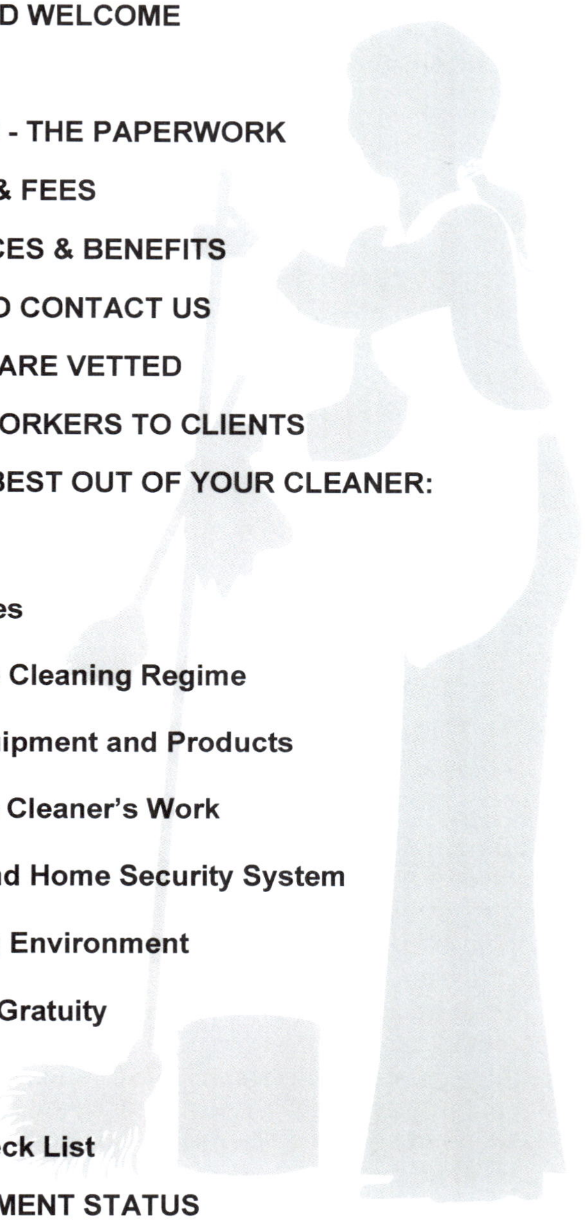

INTRODUCTION & WELCOME

Welcome and thank you for considering us to fulfil your domestic / cleaning and / or ironing needs.

This information booklet compliments the Agreement you have signed or are about to sign. It is designed to tell you how we operate and to help you get the best out of our service and the cleaners we introduce to you. We recommend you take time to read this booklet as it contains lots of valuable information and tips to ensure everything goes smoothly from day one.

OUR ROLE

(Add a small preamble about you and your business).

In simple terms our main function is to provide our clients with cleaners wanting to work in the domestic sector. It sounds simple, but in reality we have to put in a significant amount of effort to find suitable cleaners who are able to pass our thorough vetting procedures. In fact we expect 90% of cleaners applying to join our database to be eliminated as unsuitable for one reason or another. We value our reputation and will not compromise on quality.

GETTING STARTED - THE PAPERWORK

To enrol with us we need you to complete, authorise and return our Client Agreement and Bank Mandate forms, which came with this Client Information Booklet. You should send us the top copy and retain the bottom copy of the forms for your records. Upon receipt we will immediately commence the process of matching your particular requirements to cleaners on our database. If we find a suitable match we will ask them to contact you to set up an initial meeting (see Allocation of Workers to Clients). If we cannot find a suitable match we will specifically recruit for your particular needs, though obviously this may take a little longer.

OUR AGREEMENT & FEES

In simple terms our agreement is a 3-month rolling contract with a 1-month written termination notice. We believe this allows a reasonable amount of time for you to try our service whilst providing the flexibility to terminate arrangements if your personal circumstances change or things don't work out. Our fee is based on the average number of weekly hours that you contract with the cleaners we introduce. The more hours that you take the cheaper it gets per hour. It can be likened to membership of a Gym, where you pay for the services even if you choose not to use them. However, we are willing to provide a part fee refund when you notify us that you require a temporary or permanent replacement cleaner but we are unable to allocate a worker within 7 days of your request. To claim a refund, just send us a copy of the completed Cleaner Earnings Receipt Record, showing the period of absence. Our fees are paid in advance through a Standing Order Mandate, however, the form will not be sent to your bank for processing until we have allocated a cleaner to you. Once you have started a cleaner you pay them yourself, either after they have finished each cleaning session in your home, or no later than one week in arrears (see Cleaner Pay & Conditions).

OUR PRIME SERVICES & BENEFITS

1) We maintain a database of thoroughly vetted, approved cleaners in order to:

a. Provide you with a regular worker matching your needs.

Benefits:
We take the hassle out of finding and checking the credentials of candidates (see 'How Applicants are Vetted '), leaving you to simply focus on the final recruitment decision.

b. Provide you with a temporary or permanent replacement if your regular cleaner goes on holiday, falls ill or leaves. We hope your cleaner stays as long as you want them to, however, it is the nature of the cleaning industry that cleaners can be transient creatures that move on every 3 to 6 months. We are sure you do not have the time or inclination to find suitable replacements yourself and that is where we earn our fee.

Benefits:
We will do our best to supply you with replacement worker (if required) so that continuity of service is maintained. In the unlikely event that we are unable to offer a suitable replacement within 7 days of you telling us, we will refund a proportion of the fees paid until we have reallocated a cleaner.

2) We provide induction training for our cleaners to re-enforce safe, secure, productive, hygienic and customer focused working practices.

Benefits:
Cleaners are quickly up to speed. Peace of mind and quality results.

3) We provide a system that facilitates the client / cleaner working relationship and ensures that statutory requirements are addressed. For example we provide standard Task Lists, Key Security Deposit Forms, Cleaner Earnings Receipt Records and separate Guidance Booklets for Clients and Cleaners. We also monitor Cleaners' overall earnings from the work we've given them.

Benefits:
Methodical systems of work and proper arrangements for meeting IR requirements and the safe return of keys. Ensures the relationship with your cleaner is productive and relaxed.

4) We provide ongoing support to handle any difficulties that may arise. For example you may be dissatisfied with your cleaner and require a replacement.

Benefit:
You can rest assured that we are always there to provide advice, assistance and back up.

5) As a courtesy to our clients we provide certain insurances to compliment your own household policies (see full details under Insurances Section).

Benefit:
Should major property damage or accidents occur we provide a safety net.

HOW AND WHEN TO CONTACT US

Our Hours of Business are 9am to 6pm (Monday to Friday).
Tel. Number: (Add your telephone number here).
We are here to help, so please do not hesitate to contact us if you have a problem.
If we are unable to pick up please leave a message stating your telephone number, preferred call back time and a brief reason for your call. We will contact you as soon as we can. Alternatively if it is more convenient you can e-mail us at (Add your email here).

Here are some occasions when you should contact us::

1. **To confirm acceptance of cleaner.**
   Please confirm the agreed start date and if the hours have changed from those stated on the agreement. All relevant information is maintained on our database
2. **To cancel.**
   Write to our address giving one month's notice of your intention to cancel the agreement. Also write to your bank to cancel the bank mandate.
3. **To permanently replace your cleaner.**
   It sometimes happens that cleaners prove to be unsatisfactory for various reasons. Simply tell us why and we will do our best to find a suitable replacement within 7 days.
4. **To temporarily replace your cleaner.**
   Sometimes cleaners will let you down or want to take holiday. Simply tell us what has happened within 48 hours and we will do our best to find a suitable replacement within 7 days.
5. **To increase or reduce hours.**
   Please agree this with your cleaner and confirm the new arrangement to us.
6. **To temporarily suspend the service.**
   If you wish to temporarily suspend the service (for example: to go on holiday). Simply advise your cleaner, giving them as much notice as possible and confirm arrangements with us.
7. **To report accidents.**
   If your cleaner has an accident whilst working in your home, which causes damage to your property or injury to the cleaner or others. Please provide relevant details and we will advise you how to proceed (also see Insurances Section for further information).

Polite Request:
It is inevitable that you may feel annoyed if your cleaner lets you down. If this happens please do not get upset with the our staff. Please keep in mind that it is not us to blame but the worker. Simply acquaint us with the circumstances within 48 hours and we will thoroughly investigate matters by contacting the worker. We will either arrange for them to resume their duties or organise a replacement according to your wishes. We will not hesitate to take appropriate action against workers who regularly let down clients. Please remember that it is not easy to find totally reliable cleaners for the rates we recommend.

HOW APPLICANTS ARE VETTED

1. We initially carry out a structured telephone interview to assess basic suitability. This eliminates many applicants because they are either unsuitable or are unable to meet the following requirements:

   a. Proof of identification (for example passport).
   b. Proof of address (for example a recent electricity bill, in their name).
   c. Two passport size photographs.
   d. Work permit, if applicable (to demonstrate the right to work in the UK).

e. Either two written references from previous employers or, in certain situations, we may allow character references from select occupations (for example clergy or teacher).
f. We ensure that all references are verified.
g. Contactable by telephone.

2. Once the applicant has put together the above requirements, we visit them in their own home to carry out a detailed interview and verify the documentation. We choose to visit applicants in their own home as it provides proof of address in conjunction with the documentary evidence. It also gives us an opportunity to review the standard of housekeeping in the applicant's own home! As part of this process we ask applicants to declare if they have ever been convicted of any criminal offences, however, under the data protection act it is no longer possible to ask the Police to carry out checks on individuals. We do however ask applicants if they would have any objection to us running a criminal records check on them. Obviously if they are reluctant to allow this we would have to take it into consideration! If full criminal record vetting is essential to you we may be able to arrange this on your behalf, with the cleaners permission. However, the process currently takes about 3 to 4 weeks and you would need to pay fees to the Criminal Records Bureau (CRB) and one of their licensed umbrella organisations. This tends to be impractical because often by the time the results are received back the Cleaner has found employment elsewhere.

3. We then contact the referees and request specific feedback on the applicant, with particular emphasis on their honesty, reliability and work performance. We keep copies of all worker references, copies of which are available upon request.

4. After successfully completing our exhaustive checks we then ask one final subjective question: Would we be happy to offer this person work in our own home?

ONLY IF APPLICANTS PASS ALL OUR VETTING CRITERIA DO WE CONSIDER ALLOCATING THEM TO CLIENTS. WE ARE CONFIDENT OUR VETTING PROCEDURES PROVIDE A ROBUST METHOD OF FINDING HONEST, RELIABLE AND COMPETENT WORKERS.

ALLOCATION OF WORKERS TO CLIENTS

After we have received the approved client agreement and bank mandate from you we will review our database and match a suitable worker to your particular requirements. We then ask the cleaner to contact you directly to set up a mutually convenient time to meet one another. This is your opportunity to outline the work you want the cleaner to undertake and to see if you get on with them and vice versa. If you are happy with the cleaner you simply need to advise us of the agreed start date and confirm the number of weekly hours required. If you are not satisfied with the applicant, please let us know as soon as possible so that we may find a replacement candidate for your consideration.

HOW TO GET THE BEST OUT OF YOUR CLEANER

Task Lists

On your cleaner's first day we recommend that you familiarise her with your home. In each room advise her not only what tasks are to be completed but also how you want them carried out. We have included a Task List Form for this purpose. It is also very important that you point out to the cleaner any cherished or valuable items that you do **not** wish them to clean. A simple tip for specifying the work you want done in each room is to divide it into three sections and then list the jobs out:

- **Upper Level**
  For example: remove cobwebs, clean door tops, ceiling lights and fitments.

- **Mid Level:**
  For example: clean pictures, lamps, ornaments, switches, cupboard doors, surfaces and window ledges.

- **Low / Floor Level**
  For example: carpets, wooden floors, skirting boards, rugs, under furniture and beds.

Obviously some chores might be undertaken on a weekly basis whereas others might be carried out on a less frequent basis.

Work Priorities
Please be realistic when setting work tasks; this particularly applies if you have a large house but only employ the cleaner for a small number of weekly hours. You may wish to consider prioritising the Task List so that the most important work gets completed in the time available. After a few weeks your cleaner should settle into a routine, leaving you to decide if you need more or less hours to complete the scheduled work. If you do change the hours please remember to advise us.

Best Practice Cleaning Regime
Unless you provide alternative instructions we have advised your cleaner to use the following 'best practice' method of working:

1) Work from the highest level down. In this way any dust / dirt will fall to the floor where it can be vacuumed.

2) For reasons of hygiene we encourage clients to follow a colour coding system to prevent cross contamination. To employ this system you will need to provide the cleaner with appropriately coloured gloves and cloths. We recommend:

- Yellow for kitchen and food preparation areas.
- Pink for toilets, bidets and other sanitary appliances.
- Blue for other low risk areas.

Should you not wish to follow the colour coding system then please consider the supply of a dedicated bathroom / toilet cleaning kit to eliminate cross contamination from high-risk areas.

3) Always work from the cleanest to the dirtiest areas in the house, for example start with the kitchen and work your way through to finish with bathroom(s) and toilet(s).

Cleaning Equipment and Products

It is your responsibility to provide appropriate cleaning equipment, products and tools for the tasks set, including a fully working vacuum cleaner and steam iron. Nowadays cleaners are not expected to follow outdated cleaning methods such as scrubbing floors on their hands and knees, please ensure your cleaner is provided with correct and modern 'tools for the job' as this will foster a productive and happy worker.

Great care should be taken to prevent the inappropriate use of abrasive cloths and powders, which can scratch work surfaces, sanitary ware, furniture and glassware. We would recommend the use of non-abrasive cleaning products to eliminate this potential problem. Please note that our insurance policy does not cover damage to property where the client has contributed to the damage by supplying inappropriate cleaning materials.

All cleaning equipment and products are different, so please take time to explain:

- How each item of equipment works, for example how to change the dust bag in the vacuum cleaner.
- The safe use of equipment and products.
- Where equipment and products are stored.

Checking the Cleaner's Work

Please resist the urge to 'hover' around whilst your cleaner is working as this is likely to be off-putting for both of you. Also, although we want you to make your cleaner feel at home, please realise that prolonged chatting will inevitably mean that less work gets done. We recommend that you initially check the standard of work after each cleaning session before moving to less frequent inspections once you feel more confident in the cleaner's ability. It may take two or three visits for your cleaner to 'tune in' to your exact requirements and develop the optimum cleaning routines for your home. Please be patient, make a note of any deficiencies so that you can diplomatically 'coach' the cleaner before she begins the next cleaning session. We receive few complaints about the competence of workers; however, if persistent problems occur please let us know. Very often competence is a matter of personal preference.

Door Keys and Home Security System

If you are usually out when your cleaner calls, you will probably want her to hold a door key to she can let herself in. To protect the interests of clients and workers we recommend that you complete a Key Security Deposit Form (provided with this information pack) which confirms the arrangement for the transfer of keys. To ensure there is an incentive for your worker to hand back keys when they stop working for you, we recommend that you take a small deposit (say £10), which is immediately refundable in cash when the keys are returned. The deposit may be paid to you in cash or more usually deducted from the first week's earnings.

If your home is fitted with a security system and it may be switched on when your cleaner calls, you will also need to advise her how to deactivate / reactivate it.

Safe Working Environment

As a caring employer you have an obligation to provide a safe working environment. An investment of a little time and a few low cost items will ensure your cleaner operates in a safe environment and the bonus is that you and your family will also benefit from these common sense precautions:

- Maintain a First Aid Kit and show the cleaner where it is kept.
- If you have a fire extinguisher or fire blanket, show your cleaner where it is located.
- If you want your cleaner to work at higher levels, please provide a stepladder or other appropriate equipment. Do not expect them to use chairs or other inappropriate items. We recommend that 2 people are present if working above head height.
- If you expect your cleaner to use potentially hazardous chemicals (for example Oven cleaner) please provide a pair of safety goggles and protective gloves.
- Check that your electrical equipment is in good working order and electrical cables and connections are sound.
- Do not ask your cleaner to work externally (for example cleaning outside windows) as this is not covered by our insurance.

Remember that accidents can happen at any time and prevention is always better than cure.

Cancellation Gratuity

We recommend that you pay a cancellation gratuity whenever you give workers less than 24 hours notice that you wish to cancel a planned work session or the cleaner is unable to gain access to your home through no fault of their own. For example, you may have inadvertently double locked a door. In this type of situation a minimum payment of £5 should be paid to the cleaner for their travel expenses / wasted time. Please remember that wasted visits cost a lot of money relative to most cleaner's personal budget so it is only fair and proper that they should be compensated.

Pets
If you have pets please agree how these should be dealt with when the cleaner calls. A pussycat may not present a particular problem unless the cleaner suffers from a cat hair allergy, however, a pet snake may need careful consideration!

First Day Checklist
This is a useful list of topics to cover on your cleaner's first day:

- Visit each room and talk your cleaner through what you want done and how you would like them to do it. We have provided Task List forms to help with this.
- Identify any cherished / valuable Items that you do not want cleaned.
- Show the cleaner where cleaning equipment is stored and how it works, for example how to empty the vacuum.
- Show the cleaner the cleaning products you are providing and advise if you want them to follow a colour coding cleaning system to prevent cross contamination (see Best Practice Cleaning Regime).
- Confirm arrangements for handover of pay and completion of the Cleaner
- Earning Receipt Record. We recommend that earnings be handed over at the end of each work session or no later than one week in arrears.
- Complete a Key Security form if you expect the cleaner to let herself in.
- Explain how to activate / deactivate the house security system, if appropriate. Show the cleaner where the First Aid Kit is kept.
- Exchange contact information with the cleaner. You will both need to contact one another at some point in time. We have provided a form for this purpose.
- Agree any special arrangements for pets during cleaning sessions.

CLEANER EMPLOYMENT STATUS

As stated earlier our prime role is to maintain a database of cleaners, that you have access to as and when required. When we introduce a worker to you they become your employee as soon as they start working for you. This is because you are responsible for

- Setting work tasks and routines and explaining how your equipment works.
- Agreeing the times and days you wish them to work, including the total number of required weekly hours.
- Paying them directly in cash at the agreed rate, at the end of each session, or as decided between you.

An exception to this is if the cleaner has officially declared themselves as Self Employed, which is extremely rare as most workers are part time and do not earn enough money to require such action.

DEALING WITH THE 'RED TAPE'

The reason you have taken on a cleaner is to make your life easier, therefore, we realise you do not want to be bogged down with red tape relating to PAYE and National Insurance etc. Our answer is to provide the means to avoid the red tape through our worker selection and earnings monitoring system. To understand the system we must first acquaint you with the current income tax and national insurance thresholds:

- Income Tax Annual Personal Allowance 2014 -15: £10,000
  This equates to £192per week

- National Insurance (NI) Lower Earning Limit: £111 per week.

Consequently as long as the worker's cumulative earnings are less than £111 per week, you are not liable for employer's National Insurance (NI) nor are you required to collect employees NI and Income Tax.

We record and carefully monitor workers cumulative earnings from all clients on our database. If you want to find out your worker's cumulative earnings simply contact us. Obviously it is important to advise us if you increase the cleaner's hours or pay them more than our recommended hourly rate, as this will impact on our calculations. In this way we are able to take appropriate action to protect our clients interests. For example, the cleaner may be encouraged to become self-employed if it is projected that they may exceed the thresholds. Please note that It is extremely unlikely that cleaners will exceed NI & PAYE thresholds as in practice they work less than 11 hours per week.

The above information is our interpretation of current Income Tax and National Insurance information at the time of going to press. For more information we recommend you visit the following website: http://www.inlandrevenue.gov.uk/rates.

CLEANER EARNINGS RECEIPT RECORD

To maintain an accurate record of cleaner earnings and receipts we have provided you with Cleaner Earnings Receipt Record forms. You simply need to fill in the middle section and ask your cleaner to complete the first and last sections. The form must be used to record each working session. When the form is full you should sign at the bottom and pass the second copy of the form to the cleaner. Please keep the top copy of the form in a safe place, as it is a legal requirement to retain it for six years after the worker has left your employment.

CLEANER PAY AND CONDITIONS

- **Pay**
  Your cleaner relies on your income, therefore, it is important that you pay her promptly in cash after she has finished each cleaning session in your home, or no later than one week in arrears. Please complete a Cleaner Earnings Receipt Record (see above) to record all earnings and payments.

- **Holiday Entitlement**
  The holiday year runs from 1st January to 31st December. It is a statutory requirement that employers give their workers holiday pay, currently 20 days per year, plus bank and public holidays (usually 8 per year). For part time workers this is provided on a pro-rate basis,

  For the layman, the precise calculation of holiday pay for part time workers can seem like a complicated business, so we are happy to calculate this for you, if required.

- **Holiday Scheduling and Notice**
  We believe the question of when holidays are taken and how much notice either party gives is best left to a local, common sense agreement between clients and cleaners, providing **at least** one week's notice is given. This is particularly important if you want a replacement cleaner whilst your regular cleaner is away.

- **Statutory Sick Pay**
  There is no requirement for you to pay your cleaner statutory sick pay because you are paying them less than the National Insurance lower earnings limit.

- **Statutory Maternity / Paternity Pay**
  There is no requirement for you to pay your cleaner maternity / paternity pay because you are paying them less than the National Insurance lower earnings limit.

INSURANCES

One of the benefits of our service is that we operate public liability insurance policy providing the following scope and levels of cover:

- **Public Liability: £ (insert figure) per claim.** Covers personnel injury and damage for which we can be held legally liable caused by the negligence or omission of the cleaner.

The cover only operates if our fees have been paid in advance as detailed in the our Agreement.

The purpose of our insurance is to provide cover for major damage or disasters. It is not intended to cover minor accidents and low value breakages. The policy has an excess of £ (insert figure), therefore, we and our insurers cannot accept liability for claims under £ (insert figure), which are excluded. For claims in excess of £ (insert figure), you will be liable to pay the first £ (insert figure) of each claim.

Theft of belongings cannot be and is not covered under our insurances.

For full details of insurance cover and exclusions please refer to our Client Agreement. You are also recommended to check the scope of cover provided by your own household policy.

Like any insurance policy there are terms, conditions and exclusions set out in the policy document, which shall bind you in the event of a claim. We are happy to make a copy of the policy available for your inspection upon request.

REFERRAL REWARDS

We hope you like our service and might recommend us to your friends and relatives. We will pay £20 in Marks & Spencer Vouchers for each introduction you make to us leading to new clients taking our services.

Appendix D - Worker Task List:

TASK LIST

Add Your Logo Here

Please indicate priority tasks within the given time and also specify cleaning method using the following codes:

M: Mop P: Polish D: Dust V: Vacuum C: Clean O: Other (specify)

For example, please specify if you require wooden floors mopped (M) or polished (P)
Please use a seperate form if necessary if the work varies from week to week

HALLWAY	To Do Code	Completed
Flooring		
Carpet/rug		
Skirting/dado rail		
Picture frames		
Light fittings/lampshades		
Mirrors		
Doors		
Window ledge		
Windows inside		

KITCHEN	To Do Code	Completed
Flooring		
Hob		
Oven inside		
Oven outside		
Fridge inside		
Fridge outside		
Washing machine outside		
Tumble drier outside		
Microwave inside		
Microwave outside		
Cupboard fronts		
Wash up		
Load dishwasher		
Unload dishwasher		
Sink		
Work tops		
Empty waste bin		
Doors		
Window ledge		
Windows inside		

DINING ROOM	To Do Code	Completed
Flooring		
Carpet/rug		
Skirting/dado rail		
Picture frames		
Light fittings/lampshades		
Fireplace		
Mirrors		
Doors		
Tables		
Chairs		
Window ledges		
Windows inside		
Drinks trolley		
Hostess trolley		

LOUNGE	To Do Code	Completed
Flooring		
Carpet/rug		
Skirting/dado rail		
Picture frames		
Light fittings/lampshades		
Fireplace		
Mirrors		
Doors		
Tables		
Chairs/sofa		
Window ledges		
Windows inside		
Doors		

BATHROOM	To Do Code	Completed
Bath		
Shower		
Sink & taps		
Soap dishes		
Mirror		
Tiles/surfaces		
Disinfect toilet		
Bidet		
Flooring		
Window ledges		
Windows inside		
Doors		
Empty waste bin		

BEDROOMS	To Do Code	Completed
Change bed linen		
Make bed		
Pictures		
Mirrors		
Skirting/dado		
Light fittings/lampshades		
Cupboards		
Surfaces		
Carpets		
Flooring		
Window ledges		
Windows inside		
Doors		
Empty waste bin		

UTILITY ROOM	To Do Code	Completed
Sink		
Flooring		

STAIRS & LANDING	To Do Code	Completed
Skirting/dado rail		
Picture frames		
Light fittings/lampshades		
Mirrors		
Doors		
Flooring		
Carpet/rugs		
Window ledges		
Windows inside		
Doors		

IRONING	To Do Code	Completed
Dresses		
Jeans		
Shirts		
Skirts		
Trousers		

Cleaners are expected to iron approx 8 shirts per hour

Other Rooms/Duties/Comments:

Appendix E - Cleaner Earnings Receipt Record:

CLEANER EARNINGS RECEIPT RECORD FOR: ______________________ (Insert Cleaner's name)

(Use a different sheet for each new worker)

CLEANER COMPLETES					Total time worked	Sign to confirm work done	CLIENT COMPLETES				CLEANER COMPLETES (on receiving pay)	
Wk. No.	Day Worked	Date Worked	Start Time	Finish Time	Hours:Mins	Signed	Earnings Due	Pay Given Now	Date Paid	Any Amount Owed	Signed for	Date Received
1												
2												
3												
4												
5												
6												
7												
8												
9												
10												
11												
12												
13												
14												
15												
16												
17												
18												
19												
20												
21												
22												
23												
24												
25												

I confirm that this is an accurate record of payments made to this cleaner.

Signed: ______________________ (Client) Name: ______________________ (Please Print)

Date: ____________

Top copy - Client

Bottom copy - Cleaner

Important note: For legal reasons please retain this document for up to six years.

Appendix F - Key Security Deposit Form:

KEY SECURITY DEPOSIT

Your Company Logo Here

This form has been provided to record the arrangement for the transfer of property keys from the Client to the Cleaner. The Client and Cleaner may delete or amend any conditions if this is agreed by both parties.

Cleaner's Name: ______________________________

Cleaner's Address: ______________________________

____

Cleaner's Telephone Number(s): ______________________________

Client's Name: ______________________________

Client's Address: ______________________________

____

Client's Telephone Number(s): ______________________________

Date keys handed over: ____________ Type and number of keys: ______________________

____

Deposit Agreed: £ ________ (for example £10)

Deposit to be paid as follows (delete as applicable)

- Deducted from first week's earnings
- Cash
- Other (please specify) ______________

Client Declaration:

I agree to fully and immediately reimburse the deposit amount, in cash, upon the key(s) being returned into my safe custody when requested.

Signed ______________________________ Dated __________

Cleaner's Declaration:

I acknowledge receipt of the above mentioned property keys and agree to return them promptly when I finish working for the client. I understand that when I personally hand the keys back to the client my deposit will be fully and immediately reimbursed to me.

I agree to the following conditions.

a) I am not allowed to post keys direct to the client's address for security reasons.

b) For security reasons I am not allowed to write the client's address or telephone number on the keys or key ring, nor am I allowed to write the clients details anywhere else where it could be tied up to the keys.

c) I understand that if I fail to return the keys I will lose my deposit and I may also be personally liable for the cost of replacement keys and/or locks.

Signed ______________________________ Dated __________

(Company contact details here)

Appendix G - Internally Printed Items:

Cleaner Application Form.	Laser or Inkjet printing
Cleaner Task List.	Laser or inkjet printing initially, but move to litho printing as you get more clients
Cleaner Recruitment Cards (for newsagent windows etc)	Laser or Inkjet printing
Worker Information Booklet.	Laser or Inkjet printing. Use a plastic spine, available from good stationers to hold the separate pages together.
Client Information Booklet.	Laser or Inkjet printing. Use a plastic spine, available from good stationers to hold the separate pages together.
Declaration of Income Form.	Laser or Inkjet printing
Declaration of Self Employment.	Laser or Inkjet printing
Client Enquiry Form	Laser or Inkjet printing
Cleaner Telephone Pre-Vetting Form	Laser or Inkjet printing
Cleaner Interview, Vetting and Training Record	Laser or Inkjet printing
Reference Requests	Laser or inkjet printing
Client Marketing Cards Drop Report	Laser or Inkjet printing
Client Record	Either laser or Inkjet printing or recorded on a spreadsheet
Cleaner Allocation Record	Either laser or Inkjet printing or recorded on a spreadsheet

Appendix H - Externally Printed Items and Pricing:

Item Name	**Quantity**	**Price ***
Client Agreements (2-part A4 NCR form, with terms and conditions printed to reverse)	250	£115
Quarterly Standing Order Mandate (2-part A4 NCR form)	250	£79
Cleaner Terms of Association (2-part A4 NCR form)	250	£79
Cleaner Weekly Earnings Declaration (2-part A5 NCR form)	1,000	£89
Cleaner Earnings Receipt Record (2-part A4 NCR form)	250	£79
Key Security Deposit (2-part A4 NCR form)	250	£79
Client Marketing Post Cards (A6 full colour to both sides, 350 gsm)	10,000	£175
Letterheads (A4 full colour 100gsm bond)	250 500	£79 £89
Business Cards (full colour both sides 400 gsm)	250 500	£49 £59

* Prices are valid at time of going to press but may be subject to change.
* Small artwork amendments and delivery to 1 mainland UK address is included in the price.
* Prices exclude VAT, where applicable.

If you order all the above items at the same time our trade supplier offers a 10% bulk order discount.

To place your order, obtain a current quote or obtain further information please email info@howtostartacleaningbusiness.org.uk

Appendix I – Cleaner Terms of Association:

Add Your Company Details and Logo Here

TERMS OF ASSOCIATION

Add your Company Name here (The Company) provides a cleaner introduction service. Our main function is to maintain a database of carefully vetted cleaners who we place with clients requiring cleaning and ironing services. You are employed by clients of the Company who set your specific duties and pay you directly.

Please note that clients we introduce to you belong to The Company, not you.

By signing this agreement you hereby agree to the following terms of association:

1) You must not treat clients we introduce to you as your personal clients.

2) You must not at any time seek to deal directly with The Company clients.

3) You must not do anything to cause The Company to lose clients, either during your association with us or after leaving us.

4) During your association with The Company or for a period of six months after leaving The Company's database you must not directly or indirectly, without The Company's written consent:

> a) Attempt to solicit or entice away The Company's clients.
> For the sake of clarity a client of The Company shall mean a person to whom it has supplied professional services within a period of two years prior to the material date.
>
> b) Finance or otherwise be engaged or interested in any business activity competitive with all or part of the business carried out by The Company or work for any of The Company's clients, with whom you had direct contact, within a radius of ten miles from where employed.'

5) During or at any other time after termination of your association with The Company make use of any business, corporate or other name which in any way suggests a connection with The Company or any of The Company clients.

6) If The Company's fee is not paid by a client for whom you are working, we would require you to cease working for that client. In this respect there must be a degree of trust and co-operation between us. In return we will endeavour to provide you with a replacement client at the earliest opportunity.'

If any proviso of the above clauses is found to be un-enforceable it does not affect the validity of those remaining.

I have read the above terms of association and agree to abide by them together with the notes and instructions contained in the "Add your company name here Worker Information Booklet" which I have read and understood.'

Signature: .... Date: ....

Appendix J - Cleaner Weekly Earnings Declaration:

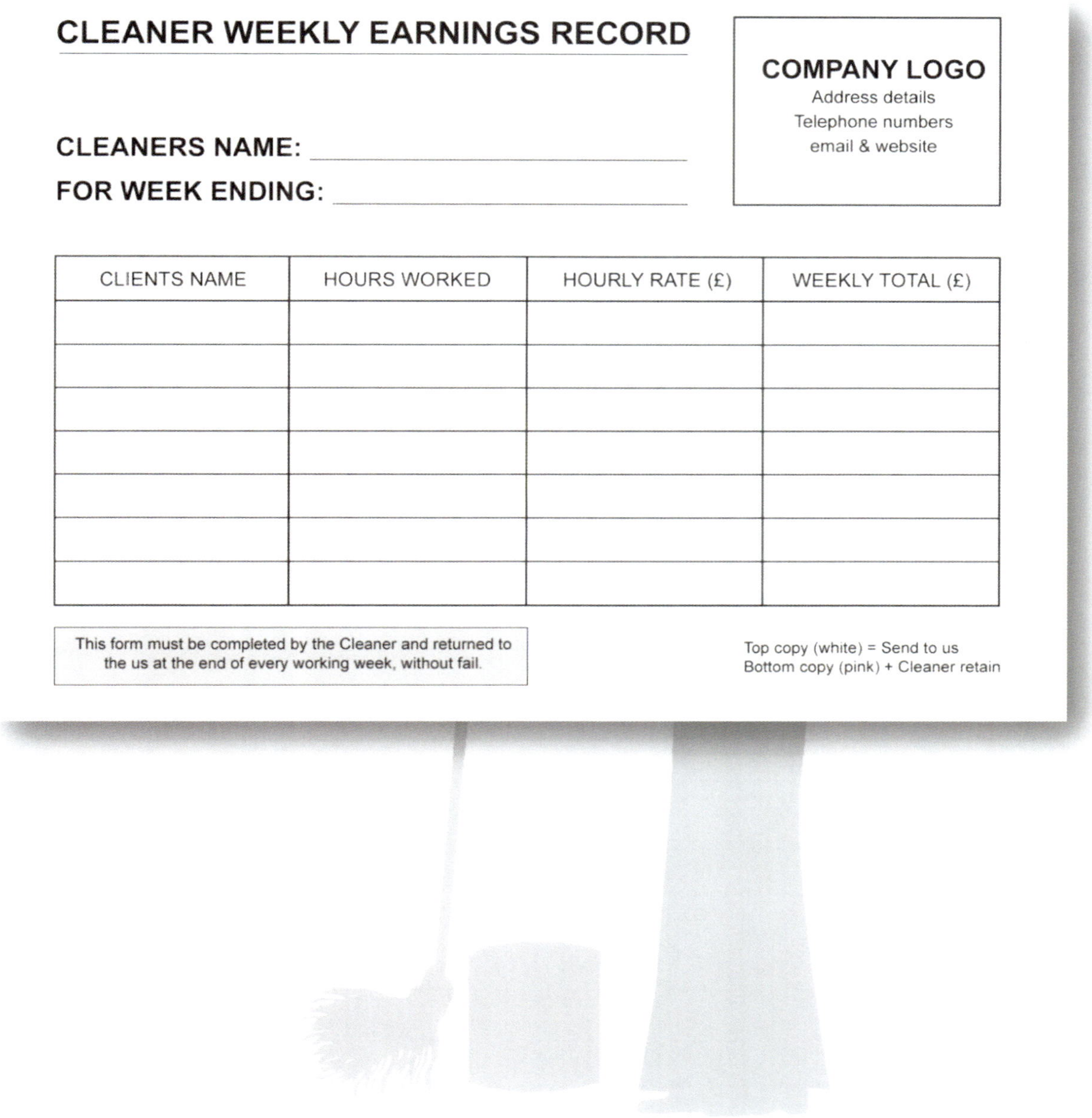

CLEANER WEEKLY EARNINGS RECORD

COMPANY LOGO
Address details
Telephone numbers
email & website

CLEANERS NAME: ______________________

FOR WEEK ENDING: ______________________

CLIENTS NAME	HOURS WORKED	HOURLY RATE (£)	WEEKLY TOTAL (£)

This form must be completed by the Cleaner and returned to the us at the end of every working week, without fail.

Top copy (white) = Send to us
Bottom copy (pink) + Cleaner retain

Appendix K - Quarterly Standing Order Mandate:

Quarterly Standing Order Mandate

Add your company logo here

Please complete in BLOCK CAPITALS

To: Bank plc (name of your bank)

Branch Address: ______________________

______________________ Postcode: ______________

Account Name: (As shown on your cheque)

Account Number:

Sort Code: – – (6 digits) (Top right corner of cheque)

Please make payments to:
Bank: (Add your details here)
Sort Code: (Add your details here)
Account Name: (Add your details here)
Account No: (Add your details here)

In the sum of: £

Amount in words:

Payable on: / / (Date)

And thereafter: £ on the day of every third month (quarter) until cancelled by me in writing.

Signature1 Date:

Signature 2 Date:

Important Note To Standing Order Clerk at the paying bank:
Please ensure the full reference below is quoted on all payments.

Reference:

Note to Client
You may wish to retain a copy of this mandate for your own records, but be sure to return the original to (Insert your company name) and NOT TO YOUR BANK, as we first have to enter in the reference shown above.

Add your company contact details here.

3827392R00105

Printed in Germany
by Amazon Distribution
GmbH, Leipzig